What's Working in
AFRICA?

EXAMINING THE ROLE OF CIVIL SOCIETY, GOOD GOVERNANCE, AND DEMOCRATIC REFORM

JESSE MONGRUE

WHAT'S WORKING IN AFRICA?
EXAMINING THE ROLE OF CIVIL SOCIETY, GOOD GOVERNANCE, AND DEMOCRATIC REFORM

iUniverse books may be ordered through booksellers or by contacting:

iUniverse
1663 Liberty Drive
Bloomington, IN 47403
www.iuniverse.com
1-800-Authors (1-800-288-4677)

ISBN: 978-1-4917-9499-9 (sc)
ISBN: 978-1-4917-9500-2 (hc)
ISBN: 978-1-4917-9501-9 (e)

Library of Congress Control Number: 2016908006

Print information available on the last page.

iUniverse rev. date: 04/29/2017

ACKNOWLEDGEMENTS

I would like to express my gratitude to the many people who were instrumental in the production of this book; and to all those who provided support, scholarly advise during the conceptualization of ideas, talked things over and all those who read, wrote, offered comments, allowed me to quote their remarks and assisted in the editing process, proofreading and design of my manuscript. Most of these colleagues read a large part of the initial draft of this book; offering me their suggestions, critiques, and encouragements that were essential in the completion of this book.

I would also like to thank my publishing staff at iUniverse; especially Joseph Elas, my editing consultant for enabling me to publish this book. Above all I want to thank Professor of Political Science and Theodore Lentz Scholar of Peace and Security Studies, Dr. Emmanuel Tatah Mentan, originally from Cameroon but currently residing in Minnesota; for reading, critiquing the manuscript; Dr. Robert Rotberg, Director of Harvard's Kennedy School Program in Intrastate Conflict and President of emeritus of the World Peace Foundation for inspiring me for his extensive writings on governance, leadership, and the role of civil society in Africa, and Dr. Amadu Jacky Kaba, who I also draw courage and motivation for his many scholarly publications in leading journals, magazines and edited books on Africa, former Vice President of the Republic of Liberia and Bishop of the United Methodist Church; Bennie D. Warner, for encouraging and motivating me to pursue my passion in writing, Mr. Abel Peniero of Ramsey County Government for his early council and suggestion in the development of this book's title; Mr. Pa Ann, a Public

Policy Analyst of Bangui, the Gambia for providing me many scholarly sources.

My thanks and appreciation also goes to Dr. David W. Jamieson, Professor and Department Chair, Organization Learning and Development, University Saint Thomas, Minnesota and Dr. Joe T. Isaac, President of AME University, Monrovia, Liberia; all of whom without their endorsement, this book would never find a scholarly path it possessed. To so many friends including my doctoral cohort family at the University of Saint Thomas and several people who encouraged me during the long and sometimes difficult process of conducting research inquiry for this book. Last but not least, I beg forgiveness of all those who have been with me over the course of the three years in developing this book whose names I was unable to mention. And finally, I am grateful to my family for putting up with me while away working on many occasions; sometime denying them quality family times to complete this book.

CONTENTS

FOREWORD

Jesse has written a fascinating *and* troubling book on the current state of Africa. It is loaded with facts, historical perspectives, and insights related to the role of civil society, good governance, development of democracies, use of violence, reduction in poverty and corruption, and economic development in these emerging nations. He takes a wide view from colonialism to present day and includes the variety of countries and stories that make up present-day Africa.

He writes as an historical and policy scholar, as well as a concerned native. This book presents a valuable case for both celebrating how far some nations have come and taking up the troubling challenge for what remains to be done, both internally, by the citizens, and externally, by caring nations. The solutions are difficult and complex and revolve around waging peace, developing effective governance, policies, accountability, and the role of civil society.

David W. Jamieson, PhD
Professor and Department Chair
Organization Learning and Development
University of St. Thomas, Minnesota

Let's face it. Good governance is very easy to define but very difficult to implement. It is similar to strategic planning; it has universal definitions and organization-specific definitions. In this book, Jesse has clearly outlined that good governance is not about results only, nor is it about development, but rather the process of making and implementing sound decisions to benefit more people and communicating those decisions to the population. He recounts the story of more than ten African countries and how they made decisions to change their fate and improve the conditions of their citizens. By the time you complete this book, you will agree that good governance in Africa does not only depend on sound leadership, which is also scarce on the continent, but good governance in Africa requires a higher level of reliability, accountability, and fair reporting.

Because of the scarcity of information about governance in Africa, especially in sub-Sahara Africa, the role of civic society is central in warranting good governance, the impact of good governance and democracy, and conflict resolution and peace building. Corruption and the general mistrust of government sometimes help to fuel this paucity of information. Frankly, the title of the book does not do justice to this very important topic and the vast discussion it contains. The book cleverly links various subtopics to serve as drivers for good governance, but the message also draws on governance and democracy. The discussions on culture, education, foreign aid, population, and infant mortality provide the context for the primary driver of the book. The section on reform and the different types of reformers seems to support a new world order on conflict resolution.

The twenty-first-century model of conflict resolution, which includes a seven-step peace negotiation of international military observation, cease-fire, limited shared governance, transitional government, demilitarization, constitutional reform, and elections, followed by some form of decentralization of social services, adds great value to the topic. This model has been tested with some success in the Great Lakes of Africa and in sub-Saharan Africa. What is wrong with this model? This book outlines that African governance is often built around the preservation of international actors and their domestic political elites. Such policy serves the interest of few citizens and tends to exclude civil society. The role of sustainability policy in increasing growth and opportunity in Africa is well articulated in the book, with emphasis on the need for homegrown solutions with long-term impact to reduce foreign dependency and increase self-sufficiency.

So what's working in Africa? Take a seat; this book will drive you through the hills of Botswana to discover the reasons why that African nation is called an "African success story." Read on, and uncover how Cape Verde became an example of peace, unity, reconciliation, and democratic reform. Then there is Tanzania, which received independence in 1961, and how that nation struggled to move from socialism to capitalism. After a short read on South Africa and Ethiopia, you will assess democracy in Nigeria and how this British protectorate has become Africa's most populated and wealthiest nation by most accounts. The book concludes with the challenges and successes of several other African nations, including Benin, Namibia, Mozambique, Rwanda, and Sierra Leone.

Dr. Joseph T. Isaac
President, AME University
Monrovia, Liberia

PREFACE

My purpose for writing this book is to bring awareness to the audience about some of the positive things that are happening on the world's second-largest continent and to demonstrate to readers of this book that Africa, like the rest of the developing world, is a relevant partner in the twenty-first century. What effects do civil societies and democratic reform efforts have across the continent? What does the rest of the world know about Africa's success stories when it comes to democracy and good governance? Besides its critical role as a major partner on the global stage, Africa is also becoming a new partner, especially for China and the United States of America. The primary purpose for writing this book is to discuss the efforts of those African nations that have embraced reforms and democracy. The title *What's Working in Africa?* was intentionally chosen to argue the point that all is not bad in Africa as is known historically. The goal is to give readers an opportunity to realize that much progress has been made and continues to happen in a number of African nations when it comes to democracy and good governance.

The question then becomes: where in Africa are democracy and good governance happening? And secondly, what differentiates those African nations from those that are doing poorly? To address these questions, readers are encouraged to read the complete book to fully benefit from this detailed account of an overlooked continent. Readers of this book will also benefit from the rich historical accounts of the continent and those nations covered in this book. Perhaps those historical narratives will set the stage for gaining an appreciation for the positive events taking place in those nations. For those with little knowledge about the social dynamics of Africa and its people, this book will serve as a great resource in understanding how the continent is evolving socially, politically, culturally, and economically. While this book was primarily written to inform its audience about what's working in Africa, a portion of the account addresses some of the challenges these nations are facing within the success stories.

This book could be of use to any professional, educator, as well as the general public interested in learning about what's working in Africa. However, with a number of African nations still struggling politically and economically to maintain stability, for those countries this book could serve as a great resource. These nations may want to ask themselves, if it is working in country *X*, why can't we make this work in our own country? This book can also serve as a training and development material for government agencies, private sectors, nongovernmental organizations, and regional organizations as a working tool.

Every author has a purpose in mind for writing; sometimes it is because they have a passion about a particular topic or the desire to leave a legacy. The motive for writing this book is primarily to balance the story, which usually tends to be about all the challenges in Africa, such as civil wars, hunger, mismanagement, etc. Discussing both, the success stories as well as the challenges, this book will enable readers to fully understand some of the positive things that have long been overlooked.

This book is structured in two sections, with the first section covering the role of civil societies and the state, good governance, US/China involvement in Africa, and the role of the African Union and regional organizations, such as the Economic Community of West African States (ECOWAS) and the East African Economic Community (EAEC). The second section of this book deals with some of Africa's success stories in terms of good governance and democracy, beginning with the most committed nations and continuing to cover those that are above average. A few examples of African nations with success stories are Mauritius, Seychelles, Cape Verde, Botswana, Ghana, Tunisia, and Rwanda. This book is an easy read because it is organized so that one can choose any appropriate section. The issues that were discussed in this book are issues that impact every African nation. Some of these nations are more impacted than others, depending on their efforts to bring about reform and democracy.

It took a total of three years to write this book. This includes the time it took to carefully research reliable information appropriate for topics that are discussed in this book, like scholarly articles, and talking to experts who have written on or have knowledge of some of the topics discussed in this book. Writing this book was very gratifying to me personally because it allowed a new level of learning about these nations, but it was also an opportunity to apply prior knowledge about these topics. As an author and human being, I learned a lot about the social dynamic of the people, their challenges, and their successes. My hope is this book will serve as a conduit and resource in mitigating some policy and governance problems. Many African nations can learn from the exemplary nations discussed in this book how to bring about reforms in specific policy areas.

Introduction

Before going into the structure of this book to guide my audience and potential readers, it is critically important to answer some of the key questions that may be raised in the mind of potential readers and buyers of this book. I assume one of those questions is "What is this book about?" Presumably, the second question might be "Why should I read this book?" This book is written for anyone who plays a role and has responsibilities for impacting organizational change, such as good governance and democracy in Africa; especially those that have a desire for reform in organizations (both public and private sectors), nongovernmental organizations (NGOs), and regional organizations. This book is also written to articulate some of the success stories about Africa that normally do not make the headlines, specifically stories about democratic reform and good governance taking place across the continent.

Often such stories do not make the media headlines, especially Western media, and instead they are overlooked. It is indeed true that many African nations face major challenges; however, some African nations have proven to be real success stories when it comes to progress in democratic reform and good governance, a number of which are discussed in this book. The desire to write this book is the result of many years of observing and reading negative narratives about mismanagement, corruption, civil wars, and other challenges coming out of Africa. While these narratives may be true about many African nations, my desire is to provide an opportunity for readers of this book to gain awareness about some of the positive developments taking place on the continent that the rest of the world does not see or know about. The purpose in producing this account is to create that awareness by articulating some of Africa's stories about political and social development across the continent. The world needs to have such awareness, especially the Western world, where most people still have no or little knowledge about what's working in Africa.

This book was also written to discuss the role of civil societies in many of these African countries on issues such as good governance, democratic reform, and other regional developments on the continent. While the role of civil society in the twenty-first century may not be new on the continent, the civil society movement has assumed a new level in holding states accountable in a number of African countries. A major portion of this book is focused on the role of civil society organizations such as nongovernmental organizations, trade unions, women's movements, student groups, etc. If you are a professional in these areas, this book will be beneficial to you. If you represent a government agency, educational institution, or nonprofit organization, this book will also serve as a great resource in your attempt to understand what's working in Africa.

I decided to write a book on this topic because democracy and good governance are the two most pressing issues that most of postcolonial Africa continues to struggle with. Although this book is primarily focused on success stories in Africa in the last several decades, Africa's biggest challenges in the twenty-first century are its ability to effectively govern itself and maintain stable democracy. Readers will discover from reading this book that many African countries are making progress in this area. The second half of this book deals with this issue by discussing the impact of reform and democracy in some of the African nations that are making such progress. In the order of commitment to democratic reform and good governance, this book presents the countries that served as exemplars in chronological order, beginning with the most successful ones on the issues of reform and good governance.

The account also discusses those countries that still have challenges in the areas of good governance and reform. This book discusses some of the foreign policy challenges in Africa, especially geopolitical policy involving China and the United States of America. Efforts to invest, partner, and work with Africa in the twenty-first century are more critical to the United

States and China than any other industrialized nations. These efforts are beginning to look like a competition or another scramble for Africa after the departure of European colonizers from the continent. If this is a competition between these two super powers, then the United States might have to work a little harder to catch up with China, as evident by the presence of China in nearly every African country. China's economic and political interests in Africa may also be an uphill battle for the United States because of the degree of intensity.

To get a detailed account of all the topics addressed in this book, readers of this book are encouraged to take a journey with me by reading the entire book to fully discover what's working in Africa. However, I would like to clarify to readers that this book was not written to discuss all the issues that face the continent. There are other relevant issues that are worth discussing, but for the purpose of this book, the role of civil society, democracy, and good governance are the primary focuses. Anyone interested in learning more about what's working in Africa in the twenty-first century will need to do additional research on specific topics of interest. Taking a close look at real developments on the continent of mixed global challenges is often overlooked, which this book fundamentally explores.

CHAPTER ONE

HISTORICAL BACKGROUND
OF THE AFRICAN UNION

THE DREAM OF UNITY: FROM THE UNITED STATES
OF AFRICA TO THE FEDERATION OF AFRICAN STATES

Overview

During the first two decades of the twentieth century, the Pan African movement started in Great Britain and the United States with African American and Afro Caribbean intellectuals and activists such as W. E. B. Du Bois, Paul Robeson, C. L. R. James, George Padmore, and Marcus Garvey. The original goal of the Pan African movement was to emancipate people of African descent around the world through the struggle for independence for African countries that were under colonial rule. In North America, the movement gained popularity in the United States in 1919 with the formation of the Universal Negro Improvement Association (UNITA), the creation of a shipping line known as the Black Star Line, and the "Back to Africa" movement, which was advocated by Marcus Garvey (Grant, 2008; Lewis, 1988 as cited in Martin, 2011).

With the return to Ghana of Kwame Nkrumah in December 1957, the Pan African movement shifted from the realm of idealism and romanticism to practical politics, with the policy objective of African unity. The key component of the Union Government of African States envisioned by Kwame Nkrumah was to be comprised of the following institutions: (a) continental economic planning that would lead to the creation of an African common market; (b) a common currency; (c) a monetary zone and a central bank of issue; (d) a unified military and defense strategy that would lead to a unified defense command for Africa; (e) a unified foreign policy and diplomacy, and (f) a continental parliament (Nkrumah, 1970, cited in Martin, 2011).

Kwame Nkrumah and his team of Pan Africanist leaders included Ahmed Ben Bella of Algeria, Patrice Lumumba of Congo (now the Democratic Republic of Congo, or DRC), Ahmed Sèkou Tourè of Guinea, and Modibo Keita of Mali. They had planned to model their school of thought or ideal of a United States of African after the United States of America. What was not taken into consideration was the fact that the American federation had a totally different circumstance compared to the plan by Nkrumah and others to make Africa the United States of Africa. The African continent at the time had a number of issues, such as colonial and neocolonial impact, cultural differences, social and political situations that were taking place in Africa at the time, and Western influence against the idea of the United States of Africa. The second school of thought was the Gradualist (or Functionalist) approach, headed by Félix Houphout Boigny of Ivory Coast, Nnamdi Azikiwe of Nigeria, Jomo Kayatta of Kenya, Julius Nyerere of Tanzania, Philihert Tsiranana of Madagascar, and Haile Selassie of Ethiopia.

THE GRADUALIST/FUNCTIONALIST VERSUS RADICAL PAN AFRICANISM APPROACH TO AFRICAN UNITY

Advocates of the gradual, or functionalist, approach to African unity wanted a step-by-step integration in the areas that are noncontroversial, such as transportation and telecommunications; joint management of rivers and lakes; trade and customs, and market integration rather than having a radical Pan African approach of immediate and total political integration (Martin, 2011). These moderate African states were reluctant to abandon their newly won sovereignty in favor of broader political unity. Other concerns the article depicts are suspicions on the part of the African leaders that Kwame Nkrumah of Ghana was planning to be a super-president by supporting a union government. Consequently, the Pan Africanist "dream of unity" was deferred in favor of the gradualist/functionalist approach. The result of the perspective led the creation of the loosely structured Organization of African Unity (OAU) in 1963, in Addis Ababa, Ethiopia. The first meeting of OAU was held in the City of Sanniquellie, Liberia. Present at the meeting were President Ahmed Sékou Touré of Guinea, the first prime minister of Ghana, Dr. Kwame Nkrumah, and President William V.S. Tubman of Liberia.

The OAU was formally replaced with the African Union (AU), which is modeled after the European Union in 2001. In a functionalist world, stability and equilibrium of social affairs is the bottom line. The moderate African leaders were not willing to support the idea of radical change in their own backyard. Many of them have struggled for sovereignty of their countries and were not prepared to submit to a centralized political system. In addition to the Pan Africanist idea proposed by Kwame Nkrumah and others in the 1960s, in recent times a number of the authors have proposed other ideas. The African Union that replaced the Organization of African Unity was proposed by recently ousted Libyan leader Muammar Gaddafi at the extraordinary fifth summit of the OAU, held in Gaddafi's hometown of Sirte, Libya, in September, 1999. At the summit, the Constitutive Act of the African was adopted.

Muammar Gaddafi was the most outspoken advocate of African unity, consistently calling for the advent of a "United States of Africa." He assumed the role of leader of the Pan Africanist movement after the death of Kwame Nkrumah in 1972. Another idea of African unity was proposed by Godfrey Mwakikagile, known as the African Federal Government. In his book *The Modern African State,* the author argues that the severity of the African predicament calls for nothing less than a closer union in the form of an African confederation or African federal government, starting with economic integration and leading to an African market and eventually a political union (Mwakikagile, 2001, cited in Martin, 2011).

Pelle D. Danabo's idea of a Pan African Federal Union is another argument to support the idea of unity, arguing that what unites Africans more than anything else are their shared cultures and geography. Included in Danabo's argument are Africans' shared and collective suffering and affliction in the modern world. A few examples are transatlantic slavery, imperialism, and neocolonialism (Danabo, 2008, cited in Martin, 2011). The solution to the African predicament, according to Danabo, is the creation of a Pan African federal state (or United African Federal Union) based on a common Pan Africa identity and society. Mueniwa Muiu's idea of a federation of African states was one of the most prolific ideas in recent times. In her jointly authored book *Fundi wa Arika*, she argues that a new, viable, modern African state based on five political entities should be built on the functional remnants of indigenous African political systems and institutions. The entity would be based on African values, traditions, and culture (Muiu and Martin, 2009, cited in Martin, 2011).

In the proposal, Africa would have one constitution and a common foreign defense policy. Africa would be divided into five super-states instead of the fifty-four countries that currently make up the continent of Africa. The proposal put forward by Muiu outlined the five new states in the following order:

- The state of Kimit includes Algeria, Libya, Morocco, Egypt, Tunisia, Western Sahara, plus the Arab population of Mauritania, Northern Sudan, and Northern Chad.
- The state of Mali includes Benin, Burkina Faso, Cape Verde, Côte de Ivoire (Ivory Coast), Gambia, Ghana, Guinea, Guinea-Bissau, Liberia, Mali, Niger, Nigeria, Senegal, Sierra Leone, and Togo, plus the African population of Mauritania.
- The state of Kongo includes the Democratic Republic of Congo (DRC), Congo Republic, Cameroon, Southern Chad, Central African Republic, Equatorial Guinea, Gabon, Sao Tomé and Principe, Uganda, Rwanda, and Burundi.
- The state of Kush comprises Southern Sudan, Ethiopia, Eritrea, Djibouti, Somalia-Somaliland, Kenya, Tanzania, Seychelles, and Comoros.
- The state of Zimbabwe includes Angola, Botswana, Namibia, Malawi, Mozambique, Madagascar, Mauritius, Lesotho, Swaziland, South Africa, Zambia, and Zimbabwe.

According to the proposal, the Federation of African States (FAS) will be called Napata. Each of the five federal states will have a key player in the decision-making process, based on population and resources. The FAS will have a federal army made up of diverse members from the five states. Accordingly, all external economic relations will be conducted by the federal government. Economic and political power will be decentralized. The people will have more input in the day-to-day activities of the federation, starting with the village councils made up of local people. The council structure will also work at the regional level with the creation of the regional council of elders, followed by the creation of a national council and federal council of president. From each of the five regions, there will be five rotating presidents to govern the federal system of government (Muiu, 2008, cited in Martin, 2011).

In 1999, an institutional evolution occurred on the continent of Africa when the heads of states and government of the OAU issued the Sirte Declaration, calling for the establishment of an African Union (AU), with the goal of accelerating the process of integration on the continent to enable the continental body to play its rightful role in the global economy, while at the same time addressing the multifaceted social, economic, and political problems with twenty-first-century globalization. In July 1999, the (AU) assembly decided to convene an extraordinary session to expedite the process of economic and political integration on the continent.

Between 1999 and 2002, four summits were held to officially launch the African Union:

> In 1999, the Sirte Extraordinary Session decided to establish an African Union.

> In 2000, the Lome Summit adopted the constitutive Act of the Union.

> In 2001, the Lusaka Summit drew the road map for the implementation of the African Union.

> In 2002, the Durban Summit launched the African Union and convened the first Assembly of the heads of states.

As a continental organization, the African Union became the Organization of African Unity, focusing primarily on the promotion of peace, security, and stability on the continent as a requirement for the implementation of the development and integration agenda of the Union.

COMPARATIVE ANALYSIS OF THE AU, EU, AND THE USA

In 2002, the AU officially replaced the OAU, which has a primary goal of becoming a fully fledged entity, like the European Union (EU) or, to a greater extent, the United States of America. But if the African Union must become a credible instrument, a number of measures will be implemented. For example, African governments will have to give up some of their sovereignty to achieve the goal of a federal African Union. The next area of consideration is governance, which most African governments still struggle with (Han, 2008; Murithi, 2005). The African Union should use the example of the European Union, which truly serves as an example for a federal African Union. As wealthy and powerful as some of the European countries are, like the United Kingdom, Germany, France, Spain, and Italy, in the international community, they still had the determination to form a relatively powerful continental organization like the European Union.

One of the reasons that made it possible, among other things, is they were willing to give up some of their sovereignty. The five European nations had an estimated gross domestic product (GDP) of $10,174 trillion in 2007; with each of the countries accounting for not less than $1 trillion. The following is the breakdown of the countries:

1. $ 2, 807 trillion, Germany
2. $ 2.13 trillion, the United Kingdom
3. $ 1, 361 trillion, Spain
4. $2, 075 trillion, France
5. $1.8 trillion, Italy.

These same countries also amount to Europe's population with a total of 306 as of July 2008:

1. 82, 369, 552, Germany
2. 60, 943,912, the United Kingdom
3. 64, 057, 792, France
4. 58, 145,320, Italy
5. 40, 491, 052, Spain (*Journal of Pan African Studies*; 2009, vol.2 Issue 8, p. 101–116).

Today the European Union is playing a major role in international relations and the global economy in full representation of its twenty-five member states. While it is true that there are concerns among the citizens, the EU also recognized that as wealthy and powerful as many of the individual states are, they cannot compete globally and effectively without the cooperation of all member states. The same is true with the United States of America, one of the most-wealthy countries in the world. Both the European Union and the United States of America decided to be a part of a larger and more powerful entity that represents the interests of all their member states. These examples should serve as motivation if the African Union can achieve its goals. Like the European Union, the African Union must be willing to compromise by giving up some of their sovereignty to the fulfillment of the federal African Union. Kurylo and Maffei (2007, p. 16) defined the word *sovereignty* as "the supreme, absolute, and uncontrollable power by which any independent state is governed ..."

The definition went further and quoted Kofman's explanation of territorial sovereignty as an "attempt by an individual or group to affect, influence, or control people, phenomena, and relationships, by delimiting and asserting control over a geographic area" (Kofman, 2007, p. 66). Assuming that the definitions (Kurylo et al) are true, African Union members will need to seriously consider the issue of sovereignty and learn a lesson from the European Union and the United States to become a part of a more powerful federal African Union. The fact is that no single African government can compete in the current global economy.

The idea of a Pan African movement was first introduced in the late 1950s by the first prime minister of Ghana Dr. Kwame Nkrumah when he called for a United Africa; he was quoted in a speech during Ghana's independence as saying, "Independence is meaningless unless it is linked to the total liberation of the African continent" (Commander, 2007, p. 425). In the last few decades, there has been a positive relationship between most African governments and the United States in support for the federal African Union, an opportunity that President Barack Obama must continue after his two predecessors, presidents Bill Clinton and George W. Bush. Both President Clinton and President Bush left a legacy of real interest and visible interest in Africa's development in economic, political, and social US policies that demonstrated genuine interest in cooperating with African development efforts. An example of that is the African Growth and Opportunity Act (AGOA), which was passed in 2000 by the United States Congress during the administration of President Bill Clinton.

The bill made it possible for many African countries to have trade preferences as a complement to foreign aid to encourage these nations to adapt free market economic reforms and expand their product coverage under the Generalized System of Preferences (GSP). The law also provides duty and quota exemptions on their exports of textile and apparel products to the US market. The law has already made significant differences in US foreign aid to Africa. Quoting the president of Uganda, "the AGOA is the best thing the West has done for Africa since independence", (Kaba, 2004, p. 21). A number of African nations have taken advantage of AGOA. Those countries include Angola, the Democratic Republic of Congo, Kenya, Lesotho, Madagascar, Mauritius, Nigeria, and South Africa; they account for over 90 percent of AGOA exports to the United States from 2001 through 2004 (Seyoum, 2007, p.523–524).

According to *The Promise of Africa Journal*, 2007 edition, there was a bipartisan consensus of a new level of friendship between the US Congress and the people of Africa in the George W. Bush administration; which resulted in many billions of dollars spent by the US government to fight malaria, fund educational programs, provide debt relief or cancelation, and many other initiatives. In 2002, the president announced a new initiative called the Millennium Challenge Account (MCA). The MCA was later changed to a new body called the Millennium Challenge Corporation (MCC). The MCC was a government-owned corporation, headed by a chief executive officer and employing both public and private sector staff. The MCC has a cabinet-level board chaired by the US secretary of state (Wikipedia, 2010). The MCC distributed $41.5 billion to Lesotho, Mozambique, and Morocco in 2007. It also awarded a $461 million grant to Mali and expanded volunteers for the Prosperity Program in 2007. Arguably, President Yoweri Museveni of Uganda was on the right side of history when he praised US foreign aid initiatives in Africa like AGOA.

HOW MUCH BENEFIT CAN AFRICAN COUNTRIES GET FROM THE FEDERAL AFRICAN UNION?

Factoring in the legacies of mismanagement by African governments in the last fifty years or more, colonialism, and slavery, the African continent is far behind when it comes to economic and other critical developments compared to other parts of the world. According to United Nations statistics, fifty countries in the world are categorized as the Least Developing Countries; 34, or 68 percent, of those countries are in Africa (Kaba, 2007; Wisner, et al, 2005). The authors argued that "a strong federal African Union is needed; as well as strategic goals created and implemented as soon as possible to begin to mitigate the immeasurable hardships that majority of the African people are currently experiencing." There are several measures the federal African Union as a continental body needs to take to solve mounting problems facing its people.

Amadu Jacky Kaba is an associate professor of sociology at Seton Hall University who has produced many scholarly publications in leading journals, magazines, and edited books; his research focuses on the economic, social, and political development of people of African descent. One of his most noted publications is the eight strategic goals for the federal African Union (Kaba, 2007). The first strategic goal is to use the Democratic Republic of Congo and Sudan to connect the entire continent by roadways and railways. The author demonstrates that for a speedy development of Africa to begin, all countries and territories must be connected. The Democratic Republic of Congo and the Sudan are Africa's largest countries in area. The DRC shares land borders with nine other African nations. The DRC is also located in the geographic center of the African continent, and the world as well.

The DRC shares a border with Sudan, which shares a border with Egypt and Libya to the north. The DRC also shares a border with Malawi, which shares a border with Zimbabwe and Botswana to the south. The reasoning is that all roadways and railways from the Congo to the other countries that share borders with the Congo must be expanded, repaired, paved, and maintained; secondly, it will bring the people together and benefit business and interstate trade. The DRC also has the potential to become the financial or business/trade center of the entire continent, according to studies. The same methodology must be applied with the Sudan. Like the Democratic Republic of Congo, the Sudan also shares borders with nine other African nations. For combating the HIV/AIDS pandemic on the continent, the author asserts that immediate attention be given to countries and regions with serious cases. He argues that the health of any society or nation is a national security concern.

The disease is causing more deaths in sub-Saharan Africa than anywhere in the world, especially in countries like Zimbabwe, South Africa, Nigeria, Kenya, Botswana, and Eastern Africa with relatively strong economies where people can read and write. Research shows most have at least high school diplomas or college degrees. To sustain and maintain the talents of those nations, there must be a strategic goal to substantially invest in its people in African nations that had populations of 44 percent or higher under fifteen years old in 2008. As a matter of strategic importance, African governments must invest in countries on the continent with very high proportions or populations of young people. Close attention must be given to the rapidly changing demographics on the continent under such demographics. The argument is simple; young people are the future of the continent. Comparatively, sub-Sahara has more young people under the age of fifteen than any region in the world (Kaba, 2007).

As of 2008, 27.3 percent of the world's population was under the age of fifteen. The following is the regional breakdown:

20.1 percent, USA
15.7 percent, EU
21.1 percent, China
31.5 percent, India
40.1 percent, Africa

On the African continent, the nations below had 44 percent or more of their populations under fifteen years of age as of 2008:

50 percent, Uganda
48.2 percent, Mali
47.1 percent, Sao Tomé and Principe
47.1 percent, Democratic Republic of Congo
47 percent, Chad
47 percent, Niger
46.3 percent, Burundi
46.3 percent, Burkina Faso
46.1 percent, Republic of Congo
46 percent, Malawi
45.4 percent, Zambia
45.3 percent, Mauritania
44.7 percent, Somalia
44.6 percent, Sierra Leone
44.5 percent, Mozambique
44.3 percent, Guinea
44 percent, Liberia
44 percent, Angola
44 percent, Benin
44 percent, Gambia
44 percent, Madagascar

All the above African nations must first be given immediate investment consideration for initiatives like hospitals, schools, and healthy meal programs for the children.

FOCUS ON AFRICAN COUNTRIES WITH HIGH RATES OF INFANT MORTALITY

The fourth strategic goal is for the federal African Union to focus on the countries with high infant mortality rates: seventy and above per a thousand live births. According to recent United Nations statistics, the African continent leads the world in the area of infant mortality. The total infant mortality rate in the world as of 2008 was 42.09 deaths per every thousand live births. Comparatively, Africa's average during that same period was 70.65 (Kaba, 2007). The following are some infant mortality rates from around the world:

6.3 deaths in the US
6.38 deaths in the EU
21.16 deaths in China
32.31 deaths in India

The following are African nations with seventy deaths or more per thousand as of 2008:

102.89 deaths in Angola
107.48 deaths in Sierra Leone
143.89 deaths in Liberia
115.42 deaths in Niger
90.97 deaths in Somalia
107.84 deaths in Mozambique
78.83 deaths in Mali
78.64 deaths in Guinea-Bissau
100.96 deaths in Zambia
89.36 deaths in Chad
99.13 deaths in Djibouti
75.93 deaths in Nigeria
90.55 deaths in Malawi
90.24 deaths in Ethiopia
87.17 deaths in Guinea
86.98 deaths in Sudan
86.02 deaths in Burkina Faso
85.71 deaths in Cote d'Ivoire (Ivory Coast)
83.75 deaths in Equatorial Guinea
83.42 deaths in Rwanda
96.36 deaths in Central African Republic
86. 83 deaths in Democratic Republic of Congo
81.29 deaths in the Republic of Congo
74.59 deaths in Lesotho
76.19 deaths in Benin

70.46 deaths in Tanzania

27. 70 deaths in Swaziland

From the list above, it is clear indication that the African Union must invest substantial resources in infant mortality, especially in those countries with the highest rate of deaths. If Africa can ever be self-sufficient in producing its own teachers, lawyers, nurses, professors, civil servants, businesswomen and men, then this strategic goal must be given careful consideration (Shabani, et al, 2008).

The fifth strategic goal for the African Union is to invest in countries with the lowest ratios of gross enrollment. Adequate education, especially higher education, is a route to success. In this century, the countries that are dominating the world are doing so because a relatively high number of their people have high school, college, or university diplomas. These nations are dominating because there is opportunity available to attend colleges or universities. According to the United Nations Educational, Scientific and Cultural Organization (UNESCO) statistics, the ratios of students who enrolled in higher education in 2006 were the following:

70 percent in North America and Western Europe combined, 60 percent of males and 80 percent of females

60 percent in Central and Eastern Europe, 53 percent of males and 66 percent of females.

25 percent in East Asia and the Pacific, 25 percent of males and 24 percent of females

31 percent in Latin America and the Caribbean, 29 percent of males and 34 percent of females

22 percent in the Arab States, 22 percent of males and 22 percent of females

25 percent in Central Asia, 24 percent of males and 26 percent of females

11 percent in South and West Asia, 12 percent of males and 9 percent of females

10.5 percent in sub-Sahara Africa, 6 percent of males and 4 percent of females

The above UNESCO's statistics may be much higher in 2016 due to natural population growth. Interestingly, a number of North African nations were included in the Arab states category: Egypt, Libya, Morocco, Sudan, Djibouti, Mauritania, and Tunisia. The ratios of higher education for those eight African countries, excluding Libya, Egypt, and Sudan, in 2006 were 14.2 percent, 13.2 percent of males and 15.2 percent of females (Kaba, 2009). The author of the strategic plan argues that the African Union must invest to increase higher education enrollment rates in these nations, especially for females since women have traditionally been behind in education in Africa. The author has carefully studied development data from over one hundred nations in the world that provide higher education for a substantial proportion of their female population who are economically successful.

The African Union must invest in landlocked African nations as its sixth strategic goal. According to the United Nations' 2008 studies, fifteen, or 48.4 percent, of the thirty-one landlocked countries of the world were in Africa. The fifteen African nations are Botswana, Burkina Faso, Burundi, Central African Republic, Chad, Ethiopia, Lesotho, Malawi, Mali, Niger, Rwanda, Swaziland, Uganda, Zambia, and Zimbabwe. A well-structured transportation system in these landlocked nations will benefit not only the farmers who need good roads to sell their products but also for traveling purposes of the general public. Adequate transportation systems connecting different regions will increase development efforts, reduce congestion in the urban areas, and allow easy movement of people.

The federal African Union must give priority to an interstate freeway to better equip its citizens to be able to move from city to city, town to town, and village to village. Bad roads or no roads have significantly contributed to difficulty in traveling in most parts of Africa, especially countries without seaports to transport goods. In West Africa road transport cost too much and takes too long; in addition to the taxes that importers and exporters must pay to move goods, transportation is the largest expense. The cost of transporting goods in West African is among the highest in the world, according to the Trade Hub's research.

THE AFRICAN FOREIGN POLICY AGENDA: THE ROLE OF CHINA AND THE UNITED STATES IN POSTCOLONIAL AFRICA

Several challenges faced the African continent in this century; one of those is formatting a workable foreign policy. As the old colonial powers (Great Britain, France, Portugal, and Belgium) retired from the continent toward the end of the Cold War, the United States and China exerted influence on the African continent. The increase in oil revenues, foreign investment, US military bases, and trade with the United States and China represent both challenges and opportunities for the continent. The question becomes, what will guide the decisions of African leaders during this most critical period? Dr. Serie McDougal, assistant professor in the Department of African Studies at San Francisco State University, has written extensively on the topic and has advanced a methodology for a united African foreign policy that applies to two of Africa's urgent foreign policy challenges: the US establishment of various African Command (AFRICOM) and the rapidly growing economic and political involvement of China.

The argument put forward by experts including Dr. McDougal is the need to develop a methodology that will guide Africa's foreign policy for the twenty-first century and a guiding framework that will guide African leaders in selecting a unified course of action. The ability of African leaders to take such a course of action will depend on priorities most fundamental to their individual countries. In Africa, there may be two different countries with very similar demographics, geography, and socioeconomic conditions. Depending on the methodology employed by the leaders, those very countries may identify different objectives, in some cases select different allies, prioritize their challenges differently, interpret their strengths and weaknesses differently, ultimately impacting the course of action they will take. The other challenge is the fact that, historically, Africa has been forced, coerced, and manipulated into adopting a foreign political methodology that has resulted in its underdevelopment and integration in the lower level of the global economic and political network, despite the tremendous wealth on the continent (McDougal, 2009).

The African continent cannot afford the absence of ideology, and the market can no longer be allowed to serve as the methodology guiding Africa's development, especially when that ideology or methodology has not benefited its people. The current methodology has put many African nations in lower-level positions in the global economy. According to the International Trade Supply report, Africa represents a mere 1.6 percent of the world trade; which suggests that economics cannot triumph or take over culture in the shaping of Africa's development. The expansion of China in Africa should create an opportunity for the United States as a strategic partner, not a strategic enemy, in the post-Cold War era. In the last decade, China-Africa trade grew over tenfold from 2000, from US$10.6 billion to US$115 billion in 2010. Most of the trade statistics result from Chinese companies extracting natural resources, especially in the oil industries (62 percent) and metals (17 percent) that are used for manufacturing in China. The United States has also expanded trade with Africa over the same period as a result of the 2000 act in the US Congress known as the AGOA. According to the US Census Bureau, America's expansion reflects the Chinese, tripling from $38.5 billion in 2000 to $113 billion in 2010, just $2 billion behind the Chinese trade record in Africa. Most of the trade initiatives consume a sizable amount of resources to manufacture and ship exports to the West.

According to the US Department of Commerce, 91 percent of US-Africa trade is oil imports, compared to only 62 percent of China-Africa trade. Working with China as a strategic partner in Africa will enhance the values and principles of global cooperation between China and the United States. The benefits for such partnerships will not only benefit the United States and China but also the African people in general. Instead, Western media and scholars tend to focus on and sensationalize the negative aspects of China in Africa, leading to the creation of myths about the Chinese presence in Africa that are mixed with realities. While some truth may hold by critics, the full unknown story of the United States, China, and Africa is often not told. The reality, according to Peter Ehresmann, an expert who has written extensively on the topic, reveals a common theme:

that the United States and Western institutions are often guilty of similar poor practices in Africa, especially when it comes to lack of cultural sensitivity, the lack of involvement of African business experts in some cases, exploitation, and monopoly in the decision-making process.

Western nations, including the United States, have often criticized China for obstructing transparency in its involvement in Africa by giving loans to African nations with a history of corrupt practices. In her book *The Dragon's Gift*, one of the few reliable books on Chinese involvement in Africa based on three decades of empirical research, Dr. Deborah Brautigam gives an account of the real story of China in Africa. The book depicts specific examples from the nation of Angola after the civil war in 2002. The Western story reveals that the International Monetary Fund (IMF) was pressuring Angola to improve transparency before giving the country loans, but China arrived in the country with no-strings-attached loans, thwarting the West's righteous efforts. Western nations are guilty of similar bad practice, as is evident with countries like Germany and France, which violated the IMF effort. First Germany unilaterally settled a debt-reduction policy, allowing German companies to return to Angola; additionally it extended the export credit. Soon after, the French bank gave another large loan to Angola. All this happened, according to the report, before the Chinese offered their loans to Angola. Followed by the German and French, United States and Scottish banks also gave loans to Angola outside the IMF.

With respect to Darfur, the Chinese were working with the Sudanese government in resolving the crisis by sending a strong message to the Sudanese government to allow peace-keeping troops in 2008 as a result of pressure from the international community. This was a very critical shift from the Chinese core foreign policy of nonintervention in local politics. It also shows the world is moving toward multilateralism when it comes to sharing international standards. With such levels of cooperation, all parties involved benefit. The United States and its agencies, NGOs, and private companies all have valuable contributions to bring to the table. The same goes for the Chinese organizations doing business in Africa. Together with African organizations, a promising and productive coalition can be formed that includes China and the United States, a partnership that will fulfill US global interest in promoting stability, free markets, poverty eradication, and cooperation in regional security and economic development in Africa. If the United States must maintain leadership in promoting democracy, freedom, human rights, and pluralist and prosperous societies, she will need to work with China, regardless of the differences in opinion on foreign policies. The Chinese have been in Africa since the fifteenth century, and they are not going away (Ehresman, 2012).

The Chinese have invested strategically in Africa and will be on the continent for a long haul. The Chinese have experimented and discovered some strategies that work, including approaches that continue to lift hundreds of millions of people from poverty in Africa, a strategy fashioned after the world's progress on the millennium development goals. The United States and Europe need to be mindful of inconsistently maintained or changing international development strategies. On the other hand, not all of China's approaches will work in Africa, though no one will argue that some have benefited the people of Africa. Have all US and Western approaches worked in Africa? The answer is no, but some have worked, which takes the argument to the question of cultural sensitivity, meaning inviting African experts to the decision-making table, as is discussed in the next segment. Some have argued that African nations should be free to find their own paths for eradicating poverty, but that path will not be the only silver bullet for Africa's poverty and development challenges. The engagement and collaboration of the United States and China through dialogue and sharing ideas and lessons learned is vital to meeting the poverty and development challenges in Africa.

AFRICA'S DEVELOPMENT IN THE ERA OF PRESIDENT BARACK OBAMA: THE ROLE OF THE AFRICAN UNION US POLICY IN AFRICA IN THE OBAMA ADMINISTRATION

The election of President Obama to the presidency further creates the possibility for such initiatives in making the federal African Union more achievable. The president, as an American whose father came from Africa, has a much greater challenge in continuing the legacy of presidents Clinton and Bush in working with African governments as they develop their societies. Kaba, author and professor, describes President Barack Obama as a leader who has the potential to contribute in uniting the following: (A) the United States (one of his biggest challenges); (B) Africa and the United States; (C) supporting the effort of a federal African Union, and (D) contributing to the east-west regions of the three Old World continents: Africa, Asia, and Europe. Another area where the president's influence will be needed as to foreign policy expertise is supporting the idea of a federal African Union to gain a permanent seat with veto powers on the Security Council at the United Nations, because the United States is one of the most powerful members of that influential organization.

President Obama will not be the first US president giving aid to an ancestral continent; the tradition goes back more than one hundred years. One example is a US president with European ancestry who helped rebuild Europe following World War I and World War II (Merrill, 2006; Williams, 2005). Merrill demonstrates that during World War II, when Europe was destroyed, the United States government spent approximately $12 billion to rebuild Europe, known as the Marshall Plan. The author argues that the president does not only have the responsibility to contribute to the federal African Union but also the responsibility to continue the new US policy of support for positive economic development on the African continent.

GOVERNANCE, LEADERSHIP, AND CIVIL SOCIETY

Robert Rotberg of Harvard's Kennedy School's Program on Intrastate Conflict argues about the relevance of governance and leadership in Africa; in his writing he discusses that governance is the delivery of highly political goods to citizens by governments of all kinds. "But more specifically in Africa, as well as everywhere else in the world, those political goods are security, safety, rule of law, participation, and human rights, sustainable economic opportunity and human development" (Rotberg, 2008, p. 1). Robert Rotberg, who is also director of Harvard's Kennedy School's Program in Intrastate Conflict and president emeritus of the World Peace Foundation, has written extensively on governance, leadership, and the role of civil society in Africa, supporting the key components this book is fundamentally centered on.

The remaining section of the book offers a close examination of many of those African countries that are strong in the areas of good governance, leadership, and the role of civil society, as distinguished from the weak countries, according to their levels of effective delivery of political goods as described by Robert Rotberg. Studies have shown that governance in Africa is improving, according to the annual Index of African Governance. In the mix is conflict, such as the Great Lakes region, the West African Spring that impacted Sierra Leone, Liberia, Côte de Ivoire, and Guinea-Konakry, and battles in the Niger Delta, where oil wealth exists in the midst of extreme poverty. The index shows that thirty-four African governments have begun delivering improved results, including advanced and committed reforms. Africa is the planet's second-largest continent and the second-most populous continent after Asia; it includes fifty-four individual countries. Western Sahara is a member state of the African Union whose statehood is still disputed by Morocco.

These most recent improvements show that multiparty systems are now more normal in Africa. Citizens of most African countries are demanding that leaders step down after constitutionally mandated term limits, with the exception of a few old-fashioned Afro-socialists like Robert Mugabe of Zimbabwe. According to the index's most recent findings on governance, the African economies are open; as a result, millions of Africans are now on the Internet and use their cell phones to pay bills and connect to the world (Rotberg, 2008 p. 9). Top governance performance ratings, according to the Index of African Governance, show that a number of African countries, many of which are small nations, have been conspicuously well managed since independence from colonial rule. Examples include Mauritius, the Cape Verde Islands, the Seychelles islands, Botswana, South Africa, Ghana, Namibia, Gabon, Sao Tomé and Principe, and Senegal. (A more detailed account of these countries will be discussed in the chapters ahead.) In each of these countries, according to the Index of African Governance, the citizens are relatively wealthy, literate, safe, free of internal conflict, and accustomed to a solid rule of law with moderate levels of corruption. Gabon is the only country in the group with low scores for participatory fairness but high scores for sustainable economic opportunity and security (Rotberg, 2007).

CHAPTER TWO

THE ROLE OF CIVIL SOCIETY AND GOOD GOVERNANCE IN AFRICA: THE TWENTY-FIRST-CENTURY CHALLENGE

Civil society can be comprised of NGOs, such as social groups, professional groups, community-based organizations (CBO), trade unions, labor unions, indigenous groups, charitable organizations, faith-based organizations, professional associations, volunteer organizations, the media, national diaspora, and segments of the private sector like market women's associations, etc. Civil society can also include arenas outside the family, like the state and the market where citizens associate for the advancement of common cause. The World Bank adopted a comprehensive definition of civil society as a "wide array of nongovernmental and not-for-profit organizations that have a presence in public life, expressing the interests and values of their members or others, based on ethical, cultural, political, scientific, religious, or philanthropic considerations."

In light of the above definition, it is necessary to assert the following: (a) civil society is not an alternative to the state or vice versa; the responsibility of the state to its citizens is still important; (b) a true, vibrant democracy cannot be achieved without the active participation of civil society; (c) good governance and development will require strong partnerships between the state, civil societies, and the private sectors, particularly in areas of decision making and policy implementation.

In the last few decades, civil society actors have increasingly become significant as forces in discourse and the creation of policies that foster peace and security around the world. Traditionally, civil society has been instrumental in redirecting policies from a state-centered process to people-centered. This people-centered belief is usually shared in regions of the world where people have experienced conflicts, civil wars, and misplaced public trust, areas where communities and the lives of ordinary people have been devastated. Examples of such communities in the last two decades include Liberia, Sierra Leone, Ivory Coast, the Democratic Republic of Congo, Sudan, and Zimbabwe.

On the African continent, civil society has a long history of being at the forefront of movements that have challenged entrenched authoritarianism, mismanagement, and corruption to introduce accountability in public policies, transparency, and democratic governance. In West Africa, for example, civil society was active in the struggle for independence in the 1960s through trade unions, women's groups, student unions, and professional associations. All across Africa, in West Africa in particular, civil societies have been an important force in ending military dictatorships, advocating for pluralistic and open societies, and promoting the concepts of good governance. In some cases, civil societies have acted as primary providers of basic social services in war-torn regions when important public institutions and state facilities were nonexistent. They have served as the only options for ordinary citizens. According to the West African Civil Society Institute, there are reports that civil societies have been accused of aligning themselves with warring factions and assuming political positions in conflict situations in countries like Liberia, Ivory Coast, Sierra Leone, Guinea-Bissau, and the Democratic Republic of Congo. Interestingly, not all civil societies have been involved in such activities; there are numerous positive contributions other civil societies have made in promoting peace and stability in conflict situations.

Civil Society and Democratic Governance: A Global Challenge in Africa

In 2002, the Development Policy Forum conference was convened to discuss the impact of the challenges of globalization to democratic governance in Africa. A total of 126 participants consisting of African policy makers, senior officials from diplomatic embassies and international organizations (based in Addis Ababa, the Ethiopian capital), well-known African intellectuals, representatives of African civil and private organizations, and other stakeholders were present. Research papers analyzing the experiences of eighteen African nations in meeting the global challenges and the role of civil society were distributed to the participants at the conference. The three issues the working groups focused on were:

1. The challenges of globalization on democratic governance in Africa
2. The role of civil society in consolidating democratic governance within the framework of globalization
3. The role of other stakeholders, including political parties, unions, the military, and the government, in safeguarding and consolidating democratic governance in Africa in the face of challenges from globalization

For the purpose of this chapter, the primary focus will be on the role of civil society and governance in Africa.

An Analysis of Accountability and Civil Society Action in Sub-Saharan Africa

According to a 2004 World Development Report (WDR), making services work for poor people, especially in Africa, is a challenge. One of the challenges is the deliverability of basic services to the people. Another challenge is leakage of public funds and poor credibility of the state to govern. Civil society action in Africa and other places has always been focused on information provision and mobilization of collective citizen action. The effectiveness of civil society will depend on incentives and flexible mechanisms within the state; this may include the structure of the bureaucracy. When it comes to accountability and civil society organization, there appears to have been a large shift in Africa among the citizens, especially in the 1990s, with the formation of village-level groups when participatory approaches emphasizing and enhancing international development paradigms were promoted through aid and adopted by various governments in delivering projects to communities.

THE IMPACT OF GOOD GOVERNANCE, DEMOCRACY, AND DEVELOPMENT:

Experts believe that there is a link between economic development, good governance, and democracy. It is also true that strong governments play an important role in stimulating economic growth; the presence of economic development promotes social and political stability. African countries should keep this in mind as an important lesson from an historical context. It should also be noted that African economic history had a totally different pattern. The economic changes created by the colonial state were never designed or intended to promote genuine liberal national economics or the consolidation of nation-states. Rather, economics functioned as appendages of their economics, heavily fashioned with preferences for their economic groups and interests. As a result, the entrepreneurs were often neither indigenous nor committed to economic prosperity. Because of the fragmentation and domination of colonial powers, they lacked the interest and stakes in building a successful national economy similar to those which had emerged in the developed countries.

CONTRIBUTIONS OF CIVIL SOCIETY IN PREVENTING CONFLICT IN AFRICA

All across different regions on the continent, civil society has played major roles in preventing conflict, including advocating against the spread of cross-country small arms, making positive contributions toward post-conflict reconstruction, ensuring the peace process yields a win-win result with participating groups, and being involved in early warning and providing appropriate responses. In West Africa, for example, the Economic Community of West African States (ECOWAS) sees conflict prevention as activities designed to reduce tensions and prevent an outbreak, escalation, spread, or recurrence of violence. The strategy of early warning consists of the systematic collection and analysis of information coming from regions of crisis for the purposes of mitigating the escalation of violent conflict, developing strategic responses, and recommending options to critical decision-making authorities.

Such decision-making actors are the African Union and the regional economic communities: The Economic Community of West African States (ECOWAS); the Mano River Union (MRU), an economic cooperative among Liberia, Sierra Leone, Guinea, and the Ivory Coast; Economic Community of Central African States (ECOCAS); East African Community (EAC); Union of Arab Maghred (UMA), and the Southern African Development Community (SADC). Collaboration between these regional actors and the African Union has been highlighted as the best practice for how to build alliances with civil society in the conceptualization of early-warning systems. Such a model has been examined by other sub-regions across Africa during the preliminary stages of developing early-warning systems. At the national level, civil society has also worked to raise awareness of the dangers of arms production and the manner in which arms can be smuggled across national borders.

According to the Foundation for Security and Development in Africa (FOSDA), a civil society based in Ghana, West Africa, has donated metal detectors to the Ghanaian Police Service in the northern region of the country to help track down illicit arms and ammunitions. In Senegal, civil society has been on the forefront and particularly active in its fight against the proliferation of small arms and light weapons. According to the West Africa Civil Society Institute, proliferation of small arms and light weapons is a major security concern. The institute estimated that 7 million of the 639 million small arms and light weapons circulating globally are in West Africa. Therefore, the role of civil society in conceptualizing early warning is vital in preventing conflict. In Liberia, for example, where fourteen years of civil conflict displaced more than a million people, civil society organizations provided humanitarian assistance and various programs before the restoration of democratic government.

In 2011 and 2012, civil society was instrumental in North Africa and the Middle East as seen in the emerging role of the younger generation of Arabs in driving and leading change in the region.

In the three North African countries of Tunisia, Egypt, and Libya, the active participation of student groups, indigenous groups, charitable organizations, and nongovernmental organizations brought about major changes in social justice and political correctness. In Egypt, young Egyptians were the driving force that brought about political transformation. Political parties like the Muslim Brothers and other organizations joined the process later. The changes that engulfed North Africa and the Middle East could not have been possible without the crucial role played by civil society organizations like human rights organizations and women's organizations.

According to the Commonwealth Foundation report, civil society organizations have contributed to development in many ways, including raising awareness and understanding of development policies, laws, and regulatory institutions; providing opportunities for ordinary citizens to communicate with governing institutions and elected representatives; giving voice to marginalized groups in society; providing enriching input into discussions about development policies and implementation strategies; suggesting and advocating for new perspectives, policies, and methodologies. Civil society organizations enable people to be more aware of what social and economic development decisions are being made, by whom, and based on what options, on what grounds, with what expected results, and with what resources to support implementation of those decisions. Civil society organizations can play a crucial "watchdog" role in monitoring the implementation and effects of national and international programs and policies by increasing public accountability efforts to promote democracy and development.

ACCOUNTABILITY AND CIVIL SOCIETY ORGANIZATIONS

Accountability from the prospective of civil society can be defined in three ways. The first type of accountability has to do with holding government and other power holders accountable for their decisions, actions, and results. According to experts, this is known as social accountability. The second form of accountability involves donor organizations that finance their work; this is known as upward accountability. The third form focuses on holding civil society organizations accountable to the people they serve. This last form of accountability is referred to as downward accountability. When it comes to holding government and other power holders accountable, there is much enthusiasm and energy. But when the finger is pointing at the people and their own accountability, it becomes a challenge. Accountability also means being accountable to the mission and values of the organizations and groups. The mission accentuates the identity of the organization, why it exists and whom it serves. The values, on the other hand, explain what behaviors the people must embrace in order to serve their citizens better.

Experts have identified four key developments as driving forces behind social accountability, not just in Africa but in the world in general.

1. The decentralization and structural adjustment reforms that have been implemented in governments, particularly on the African continent
2. The antipoverty strategies that many African governments adopted in the 1990s
3. A history of poor service delivery
4. The need to fight corruption

The above trends have led to the creation and revival of civil society services on the continent of Africa.

CHAPTER THREE

CONFLICT RESOLUTION IN THE GREAT LAKES REGION

One of the regions in Africa that has endured many years of civil unrest is central Africa, comprised of the Democratic Republic of Congo (DRC), formerly known as Zaire, plus Rwanda, Burundi, Tanzania, and Uganda. The region, commonly known as the Great Lakes Region of Africa, has been the arena of civil unrest since the 1960s. Since the period of independence, there have been arenas of civil conflict from one regime to the other. Because of the historical significance of the region, this chapter is primarily focused on the efforts to bring about peace and reconstruction, a process that, according to experts, is fashioned by contemporary conflict resolution models with a standard formula for peace negotiations consisting of cease-fire agreements, transitional governments, demilitarization, constitutional reform, and democratic elections. According to a recent *Third World Quarterly* report, there have been a total of eleven outright civil wars in the Democratic Republic of Congo, five civil wars in Burundi, and two civil wars in Rwanda. The report does not include what is called by experts as constant low-intensity warfare in the region.

It is estimated four million people have lost their lives as a result of these conflicts, and an additional four million have been forcibly displaced from their homes, in some cases living as refugees in neighboring countries. An example is the 1994 Rwandan genocide, which took the lives of 750,000 Tutsi and marked the most tragic moment in the history of that region, as well as the international community, when it comes to crimes against humanity. Between 1998 and 2000 another civil war in the DRC involved seven African counties. The DRC's conflict was known as Africa's First World War. Because of the intensity of the conflict, it signaled the end of the principle of noninterference in the internal affairs of member states. One of the models that has been used in resolving conflict around the world is the contemporary conflict model, with a standard formula of peace negotiations, cease-fire agreements, transitional governments, demilitarization, constitutional reform, and democratic elections.

Despite the signing of the peace agreement in Rwanda (1993), Burundi (2000), and the DRC (2000) and the deployment of UN peacekeeping missions, United Nation Operations in Burundi (ONUB) and MUNOC, permanent peace has not yet returned to the region. Reviewing the peace process in the Great Lakes region, the argument experts have made is to push the standard peace formula, while recognizing that governance and structural violence are at the root of the conflict in the region. The models have failed to address the complexity of African politics and the underlying economic conditions of the people that usually are contributing factors to violence. The review also depicts the conduct of peace negotiations as reinforcing the view that African politics is the preservation of the international actors, the domestic political elites, and armed movements that serve the interests of the domestic political elite and exclude the civil society and the masses of the people.

It is therefore fair to argue that universal conflict resolution models have not resulted in fruitful outcomes on the African continent, whether in the Great Lakes region, West Africa in the case of the Liberian civil war that lasted for fourteen years and spread to Ivory Coast and Sierra Leone, or other parts of Africa. To the credit of the international community, that is at least the best model in resolving conflict. With respect to the African continent, it is unclear whether that model for resolving conflict, especially civil war, is culturally appropriate. There are African leaders, like former South African president Thabo Mbeki and other leaders, who have argued that African problems should be solved by Africans with an African personality, meaning doing so the African way: talking about our cultures and traditional values, be it dealing with conflicts in the Great Lakes, West Africa, or other conflicted areas on the continent.

THE NOTION OF PEACE

The conventional definition of peace making in a war situation is to bring it to an end by reconciling and establishing civil order among the parties involved. A peaceful society is one in which conflict is resolved by means of compromise and where the rule of law is effective, eventually providing a condition of stability. The question is, why is it that most of Africa has problems with instability? Among other issues, the African political elite has shifted to ethnicity to ensure their political survival and continued accumulation of wealth. Scholars and peace theorists, such as Johan Galtung, have argued that the concept of "structural violence" is a major cause of poverty and powerlessness that results indirectly in violence; outright violence leads to civil wars in regions like the Great Lakes and West Africa.

Johan Galtung and many peace scholars who have written about peace and reconstruction assert that social justice is an ideal perfection of social condition. The concept of peace is not a reduction in direct violence, according to experts, but a response to social injustice, which is prevalent in most regions in Africa. According to the United Nations, one of the organizations that utilize liberal and mechanistic concepts of peace given their many engagements around the world, interprets the concept as having many components. For example, peacemaking, which it refers to as the use of (A) diplomatic means to persuade parties in conflict to cease fire and negotiate a peaceful settlement; (B) peace building, which it defines as all external efforts to assist countries and regions in their transitions from war to peace by including all activities and programs designed to support and strengthen these transitions. Peace building and reconstruction are inextricably bound; they go together, yielding a return to a state of security and stability, reassuring the people and the world it's safe to do business, like investments, trade, and engaging in international relations with other nations.

In the case with some of the Great Lakes nations, to reconstruct a just society without politics liberal organizations like the United Nations and NGOs have been forced to go back to the precolonial era to revive the mechanisms for peace, such as the *ubashingantahe* in the case of Burundi and *gaccaca* in Rwanda—traditional collective organizations that recognized the humanity of people and draw a line around the rights of individuals within the society. However, one has to be cautious in recognizing the traditional African values within the society and not instituting premodern injustices that may be embedded in the institutions.

HISTORICAL BACKGROUND TO THE GREAT LAKES CONFLICTS

It will be impossible to give a detailed account of the conflicts in the region in one chapter. There has been extensive research and literature about the actual events by scholars and experts in recent years; it would take a book to cover the history of the Great Lake conflicts. Three of the five nations of the region, Rwanda, Burundi, and the Democratic Republic of Congo, have experienced violent conflicts at different levels since colonial rule; but the intensity of the conflicts can be traced to the time of independence in the 1960s. Rwanda and Burundi had a similar history to most nations in Africa, according to the *Third World Quarterly* 2006 report. The ethnic composition of 80 percent Hutu, 15 percent Tutsi, and 5 percent Twa has been documented by experts as the primary cause of the conflicts. An example of socially constructed identities can become salient and problematic, usually seen among various ethnic groups in Africa.

One major factor is the racial ideology of the colonial and postcolonial state as a mechanism for social control and exercise of state power in the ethnicity of Hutu, Tutsi, and Twa. From 1959 to 1994, the Hutu dominated political power in Rwanda, and in Burundi the Tutsi have remained in control of the country since independence in 1962. In Rwanda, the postcolonial history was relatively peaceful, but excluded the Tutsi group from power and the strengthening of the military. Regime change happened when members of the Hutu elite began to run for power. The coup of Major-General Juvenal Habyarimana in 1973 strengthened the Hutus position, followed by further purges of the Tutsi in key institutions of Rwanda. The full-scale civil war occurred from 1990 to 1994 due to the failure of the Rwandan state to recognize the legitimate right of its citizens, in exile to return, and to introduce measures for ethnic equity.

Consequently, the Tutsi-dominated Rwandese Patriotic Front managed to stop the genocide and capture the state, but it continues to be threatened by the Hutu militias that carried out the genocide. The nation of Burundi has been the scene of low-intensity of conflicts, according to experts, since the 1960s; however, in 1972 an estimated 250,000 died in genocidal killings. In 1988, an additional 80,000 died, not including those who were killed in minor fights between small bodies of troops. According to the United Nations Office of Human Rights Commission, over 300,000 were estimated to have been killed in the civil war that began in 1993 after the assassination of the country's democratically elected Hutu president Melchior Ndadaye. The Tutsi-dominated military and men at arms have played critical roles in instigating violence in the country.

As in most of Africa, unemployed young men were mobilized into ethnic militias and other paramilitary groups, escalating the problem. Factions within the political elite and the rebel groups led to the rapid increase of political parties and rebel movements in the country. It is reported that 50 percent of all military personnel in Burundi are from opposition groups (Patricia, 2012). The military action against the rebels and their supporters has led to the forced removal of 16 percent of the population from their villages, accompanied by widespread violence against civilians.

THE PROCESS OF PEACEMAKING IN THE GREAT LAKES REGION

According to experts, many international and regional organizations have acted as brokers of peace in Africa, including the Great Lakes region. Usually, external intervention to resolve conflicts in Africa is often too late or too little. An example is the Rwanda conflict in the 1990s, no matter who was involved in the intervention. With respect to the United States, there are a number of national security concerns that usually stand in the way; what is the exit strategy once America's young men and women are put in harm's way? Are there credible regional partners to share the cost? What is the national security interest to justify intervention when body bags begin to arrive home? These questions are not just for the United States but for any international and regional organizations charged with responsibility for peacemaking in conflict spots around the world.

On the African continent, there are three main factors that must be considered in peacemaking. First, the principles in the 1969 OAU, now African Union (AU), charter of noninterference in the internal affairs of member states and respect for territorial integrity is partially blamed for the foot dragging that precedes most peacemaking efforts in Africa. However, in the 1990s, the OAU introduced its mechanism for conflict prevention management and resolution; the organization, now the AU, replaced the resolution in 2002 to set up a Peace and Security Council. The second factor in peacemaking in Africa is the fact that troops from independent African states (as in the case of the Congo crisis in the 1960s) never commit adequate resources to support regional missions. In spite of all challenges, the African Union has been active in three regional initiatives for peace in the Great Lake states: Rwanda in 1993, Burundi in 2000, and the Democratic Republic of Congo in 2000.

The AU has also spearheaded peacekeeping missions in the form of the National Military Observer Group (NMOG) in Rwanda, Ethiopia, and Mozambique and the AU/UN mission in the Congo before the UN's mission (MUNOC). Other challenges are lack of funds and poor logistical support which are reducing the effectiveness of regional missions, often handed over to the United Nations, whose restrictive mandate and poor local and cultural expertise further complicate the problem. The third and final factor leading to the delay has to do with duplicitous roles (in other words, deception—pretending to feel and act one way while acting another) in the international community. According to *Third World Quarterly* magazine, Western governments have a history of being implicated in conflict in the region. An example is the 1960s Belgian colonial regime, when expatriate Europeans supported the secessionists in the Katanga region in the Congo.

The United Nations and US intervention was very much against the popular Patrice Lumumba, first prime minister of Congo, for fear of him receiving support from the communist regime in the Union of Soviet Socialist Republics (USSR). According to historical accounts of the Katanga secession, Prime Minister Lumumba's assassination was carried out by Belgian and Congolese forces with the knowledge of Western governments. The French government was heavily implicated in the Rwanda genocide because of France's support of the Rwandan government by supplying weapons for a supposedly humanitarian mission. The French government created a safe haven under Operation Turquoise to enable the perpetrators to escape. According to experts during the conflict, France acted unilaterally or under the umbrella of the European Union.

The processes of peace and security are high on the agenda of many international development organizations and Western governments, which sometimes take initiatives that are outside of the protocol of the United Nations and the African Union peace process, attempting to broker deals that will increase their influence with post-conflict regimes. There are times when regional states, like the European Union, the United States, Canada, other European nations, religious organizations such as the Catholic Church and international and regional NGOs, have acted unilaterally, all actively engaged in negotiations in the interests of peace in the region. The challenge is that each of these has its own agenda for seeking peace in the region, while operating in an opportunistic way and necessarily coordinating their efforts to benefit the region. Many times, NGOs tend to take on the role of mediators between state and civil society. Even in the area of post-conflict reconstruction, the private sector, including security firms and multinational corporations, are involved in drawing up blueprints for postwar societies, making peace a very profitable industry in the region.

CHAPTER FOUR

DECENTRALIZATION AND STRUCTURAL ADJUSTMENT REFORMS

Most African countries have adopted decentralization as a way of governance. The problem is lack of implementation; consequently, decentralization has not enhanced public service delivery due to lack of accountability. Experts believe that in much of Africa there has been and continues to be more upward accountability than downward accountability (Isooba, 2005, p. 46). In Uganda, for example, public accountability moves in an upward direction, which means toward the direction where the money is coming from. The Ugandan situation is pretty the same as in most African countries, where local government officials are accountable to the central government, the provider of funds. Government officials see little reason to be accountable to local people because they do not have influence.

The poor performance of structural adjustment reforms has led to the creation of more civil society organizations in countries like Tanzania, which has developed the Gender Budgeting Initiative program. The Tanzanian Gender Network program was created to campaign for decentralization of the budgeting process to promote more gender sensitivity in the budgeting process. On the contrary, strengthening civil society organization in countries like Ghana has led to the alienation of local government and civil organizations and tends to undermine the longer-term aim of building the rights of citizen (Mohan, 2002, p.146).

ANTI-POVERTY STRATEGIES

The second initiative on social accountability is a poverty reduction strategy, which was instituted by the World Bank and the IMF in the 1990s. The process was intended to be participatory, allowing civil society organizations to play a key role. The policy led to the creation of many social accountability initiatives in Africa. An example is the October 2000 civil society in Zambia, which has galvanized itself by forming an NGO network known as the Civil Society for Poverty Reduction (SCPR). The primary goal of the SCPR is to have more meaningful interactions with government and provide systematic and compelling inputs to the poverty reduction strategy process (Mpepo and Schamani, 2005, p.59). In 2001, the Social Enterprise Development of West Africa formed the HPC Watch to mobilize the Ghanaian civil society organizations to move in a similar direction by demanding transparency and equitability in the distribution of the Heavily Indebted Poor Countries (HIPC) fund.

PUBLIC SERVICE DELIVERY AND MILLENNIUM DEVELOPMENT GOALS

The third development driving force has to do with the tremendous challenges most African nations faced in meeting the millennium development goals and the realization of poor service delivery that has negatively affected a number of social accountability initiatives in the past two decades. In 1994, for example, a civil society organization formed the Civil Society Coalition for Quality Basic Education (CSQBE) in Malawi. The goal of the initiative was to improve eroding standards of basic education in that nation after the introduction of free primary education through tracking and monitoring expenditures on education to ensure that adequate funds are made available and appropriately used. Similar programs and policies were established in Tanzania and South Africa.

CORRUPTION AND GENERAL MISTRUST OF GOVERNMENT IN AFRICA

The fourth form of development initiatives on social accountability has to do with the misuse of public funds by public servants and politicians, the most rampant activities affecting development on the continent. In addition, most elections are rigged, leaving a good proportion of the population with feelings of disillusionment, strengthening the mistrust in their governments in general; corruption and general mistrust are the next major concerns. Most African governments do not enjoy the legitimacy required by the people because of failure to win elections with at least 50 percent of the vote. While it is true that laws are on the books by the government to strengthen the democratic process, such as anticorruption bureaus and the office of the ombudsman, most of these structures are toothless due to lack of implementation.

For instance, the Center for Budget Advocacy (CBA) was established in Ghana to provide information on the budgeting process to local people because government had shown little interest in demonstrating transparency in the budgeting process and letting ordinary people participate in the process. Another example is the Malawi Economic Justice Network (MEJN) established in Malawi with a primary function to provide economic and budgeting literacy. In other African countries, many such initiatives were formed to bring about transparency and accountability.

THE ROLE OF MASS MEDIA

Media organizations, such as radio and newspapers, have played a potential role in exerting their influence on a large number of citizens, especially the poor. In various parts of Africa, donor organizations have been involved in setting up and supporting community radio to broadcast public interest programming to enhance democratic values, human rights, and the importance of health and education. While the role of media in Africa has been noticeable, evidence of its impact is very minimal. A recent assessment of work in the nation of Benin had a surprising conclusion for the advocates of community radio. According to Keefer and Khemani (2011a, 2011b), greater access to community radio in Benin is not associated with the ability of citizens to extract greater benefits from their government. Rather, the impact of radio programming seems to persuade people to invest more of their own private resources into the education of their children and the health of their family.

Experts argued that this useful role by the media in Africa on development initiatives has no relation to accountability challenges.

Contrary to the evidence of the post-Depression era in the United States, when radio had just begun to spread throughout the nation, greater access to radio enabled citizens to receive greater accountability from the government welfare spending (Sromberg, 2004). This is in contrast to the African experience in Uganda and other parts of Africa when media was used to primarily disseminate information about leakage of public resources; in such cases, they were instrumental in stimulating public opinion and action to reduce such leakage. This clearly suggests that investments in building media capacity alone and advocating independence from the state may not be sufficient to achieve greater accountability; rather, investment in well-designed messages seems key, either those that can enable citizens to coordinate on policy performance or those that are endorsed by the state in an effort to improve efficient in its public spending.

On the other hand, there are those who argue about the role of accountability in mass media, suggesting that media could be used for political "posturing" and "pandering" to reduce incentives to pursue actions that contribute to broad public good. A typical example is when there is uncertainty about the effects of different policies, when "expert" policymakers or politicians have access to more private information about these different effects than do voters; then media coverage may induce politicians to take positions that cater to voter beliefs, ignoring the private information that could lead to better policy decision.

CHALLENGES

One of the challenges in public actions on the African continent is the issue of accountability. Civil society organizations are not excluded when it comes to accountability. In sub-Sahara Africa there has been a significant shift in activities in civil society organizations among citizens. An example is village-level group formation, which has dramatically increased over the last decade when participatory approaches have been emphasized in international development through aid adopted by African countries to deliver projects to communities. According to Bernard et al (2008), there was rapid proliferation of village organizations in a sample of villages in Senegal and Burkina Faso between 1980 and 2002. By 2002 in Senegal, according to experts, 65 percent of the sample villages had at least one village organization (from 10 percent in1982); in Burkina Faso during that same period, 91 percent had one village organization (from 22 percent in 1982).

When it comes to households, 65 percent in Senegal and 57 percent in Burkina Faso were involved in some type of village organization. The challenge with such donor-driven initiatives is that members are more likely older and tend to have more land wealth, according to Arcand and Fatchamps (2008). In rural Kenya, for example, a similar program is administered to provide leadership training and agricultural inputs to small self-help organizations that mainly serve women. The challenge with such programs is that the more educated and those more likely to have formal sector income form the greater representation of its membership. Contrary to the programs in Senegal and Burkina Faso where participants are older citizens, the Kenyan group membership and leadership moved into the hands of younger and better-educated women.

Consequently, the Kenyan programs have shown unimpressive results in productivity gains. The above examples show that accountability is still murky in analyzing the role of civil society organizations in Africa. The questions that must be addressed are public choice and the power of organized special interests that have been blamed for distortions to growth-promotion. One tragic example of conflict of interest in analyzing the role of civil society in Africa is the Hutu mobilization (and the media) in the Rwandan genocide in the 1990s.

THE LACK OF CULTURAL COMPETENCE IN SUSTAINABLE DEVELOPMENT

One of the major challenges in the administration of development aid in Africa is the absence of Africans at development planning tables in Western countries where many of the policies are formulated. It is essential to argue that one cannot develop a village or community, or for that matter a country, without its culture; therefore, it is increasingly imperative that this component (culture), which is usually missing, be considered. Besides the problem of too few African representatives—in some cases nonexistent—there is usually the issue of mismatched skill sets in meeting the development needs. An example is the murkiness between humanitarian relief efforts and sustainable economic development efforts. The skills needed for humanitarian relief, such as delivery of food and water to famine-stricken parts of the world, are fundamentally different from the skill sets needed to promote long-term economic development efforts that must be driven by a strong sector and a Non-Governmental Organization (NGO).

The lack of skill matched to economic development is clearly evidenced by the limited business experience of many large international NGO consultants in Africa. A number of these international NGO consultants have never worked in the private sector in business development, marketing, or management capacity. A few of these consultants possess the knowledge to apply business concepts within an African context, according to research from American Foreign Policy Interests, 2010. More troubling information from the studies includes the fact that many of these "experts" lack the fundamental understanding of the cultural competence necessary for sustainable economic development in Africa. That lack of coherent practices in the current framework is one of the reasons that development projects sometimes fail. This trend will continue until development aid agencies and international NGOs recognize the deficiency and make the necessary changes to correct the situation. One of the remedies is by engaging more Africans with necessary business and cultural knowledge in the implementation and design of development programs. Generally, there is no special cultural way, for instance, to drink water or to eat food when somebody is thirsty or hungry.

When it comes to cultural knowledge and understanding of local customs, there is a difference between the significant role of long-term economic development and the reduction of poverty as a goal. In his speech to the Ghanaian parliament in July 2009, President Obama underscored the fundamental truth when he said the following: "We must start from the simple premise that Africa's future is up to Africans" (Johnson, 2010). The president drew applause when he remarked, "By cutting costs that go to Western consultants and administrations, we want to put more resources in the hands of those who need it while training people to do more for themselves rather than depending on the state for everything." The president was referring to Africans taking ownership of responsibility.

The following observations should be noted when it comes to making change in community development in Africa: first, there is a need to reduce Western consultants, to be replaced with local African implementers who possess the appropriate cultural skill sets and closer to the issues. Using local African implementers is also less costly.

The second observation is the need to build sustainable local capacity and human capital to enable more Africans to do more for themselves to mitigate their dependency on foreign aid. The views of most Africans, including former South African president Thabo Mbeki, are that the solutions to African problems should be provided by Africans themselves. To provide cultural proficiency in sustainable development in Africa will require realistic cultural and local situational awareness rather than allow outside consultants to unilaterally make decisions without involving the cultural skill sets of African professionals. The involvement of African implementers and leaders in the refinement, development, and incorporation of homegrown solutions into development programs will yield greater benefits to the people who are fundamentally affected by those decisions.

Studies have shown that there is usually local discontent due to the failure of many projects after the departure of outside consultants. The failure is the result of these consultants neglecting to seek the involvement of local beneficiaries in the first place. In most cases, the failure of projects is due to little or no interest in continuing the projects or unwillingness to transfer sufficient local capacity-building skills needed during the implementation process to enable continuity of those projects. The long-term impact is increased dependency on foreign aid rather than providing the necessary skill sets to enable beneficiaries to be self-sufficient. To ensure sustainable development efforts in Africa, the appropriate variables must be available.

The best way to feed someone is to teach the person to fish for himself, not to fish for him. That is one of the majors problems in Africa, coupled with other issues like corruption, mismanagement, nepotism, etc. The argument by experts to diversify development consultants to include African implementers in leadership is very vital; such ideas will bring totally new perspectives, insights, and cultural relevance to development projects.

THE SIGNIFICANCE OF POLICY

Experts have also argued for the significant role public policy plays in the equation. Both Western and African governments must play vital roles in promoting policy considerations. On one hand, Western governments should open up their markets to more African products and encourage more in-country value-added processing before products are exported, as one expert put it. In 2000, the US Congress enacted a law known as the AGOA to provide duty-free access to a large number of products from a select group of African economies in order to increase trade between the United States and Africa. However, there are limitations for some African nations to fully participate in the opportunity because they lack capacity to do so.

Policies should also be put in place to promote and encourage foreign investment for US firms to go beyond extractive industries, such as oil, gas, and mining, in countries like Angola, the Democratic Republic of Congo (DRC), and Nigeria. A policy should be put in place to support the millennium development efforts to reduce extreme poverty in all its forms in sub-Sahara Africa, a policy that is consistent with US national security interests in Africa. African governments, on the other hand, have a much greater role to play in the process. They must create a user-friendly environment that encourages rather than discourages local and foreign investment and eliminates often cumbersome and unnecessary procedures required to establish businesses and obtain licensures to operate in most African nations.

African governments must also increase their efforts to promote and strengthen regional cooperation and economic integration. They must encourage intra-country trade activities to build their economies. A few of the institutions that will make such an idea a reality are the Economic Community of West African States (ECOWAS) and the Mano River Union (MRU), which currently serves Sierra Leone, Guinea, Liberia, and the Ivory Coast. Part of the ECOWAS plan is to create a common currency to be called the eco by 2015. Once this plan is implemented, the initiative will lead to increased currency stability and help promote long-term regional economic growth. In other parts of Africa, similar ideas are being implemented to bring about economic integration (Johnson, 2010).

CHAPTER FIVE

PANORAMIC VIEW OF
AFRICAN DEMOCRACY:
"A GLASS HALF FULL"

CLASSIFICATION OF AFRICAN COUNTRIES ACCORDING TO
LEVEL OF CIVIL SERVICE REHABILITATION EFFORTS.

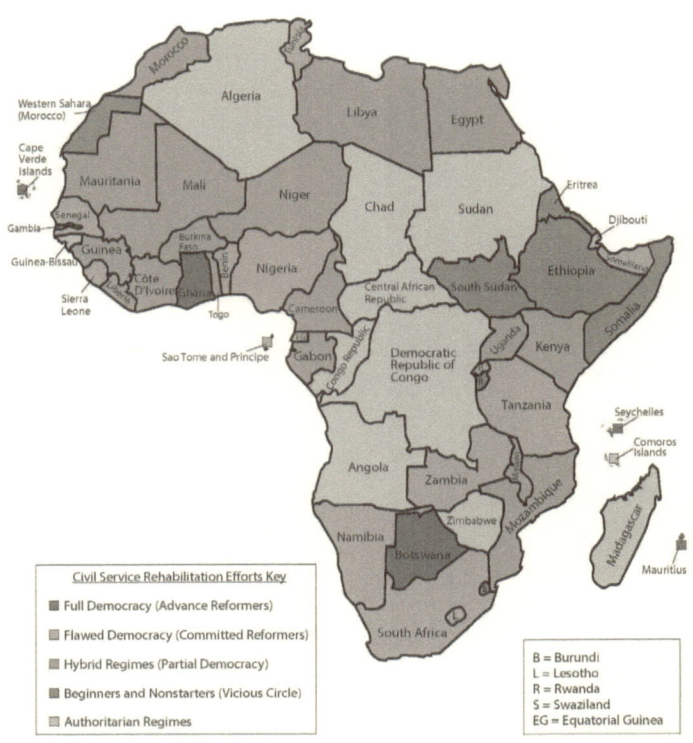

Civil Service Rehabilitation Efforts Key

- ■ Full Democracy (Advance Reformers)
- ■ Flawed Democracy (Committed Reformers)
- ■ Hybrid Regimes (Partial Democracy)
- ■ Beginners and Nonstarters (Vicious Circle)
- ■ Authoritarian Regimes

B = Burundi
L = Lesotho
R = Rwanda
S = Swaziland
EG = Equatorial Guinea

Designed By Ernest S. Norris •Photo Shop Studio 7710 Brooklyn Blvd. Minnesota • 612-408-5160

The map above demonstrates that there is still a long way to go for full democratic process in Africa. Research findings about reform efforts placed African countries in six categories: full democracy, flawed democracy, hybrid regimes, authoritarian regimes, failed states, and no data (*African Democracy*, 2011). However, reformers are hopeful that progress has been made in a number of countries, as indicated on the map. Mauritius is one of the only full democracies in Africa. While it is true that the glass is half full when it comes to democratic reform, one can argue that a number of countries are making progress. Many wonder which way African politics will head in the twenty-first century. Will it take the path of Senegal, where its president conceded in an electoral defeat to a younger rival, extending what is considered a democratic tradition unbroken since the country's independence in the 1960s? Or will African politics in the twenty-first century be like Senegal's nearby neighbor Mali, where a few days before the Senegal electoral process, a group of junior army officers stormed and looted the Malian presidential palace in the capital of Bamako, ending abruptly the twenty-year democracy that raised hopes in Mali and the wider region.

Democracy in sub-Sahara Africa is taking an increasing downturn, while at the same time electoral contests and term limits are accepted as fixed rules. Many Africa watchers perceive a gradual erosion of the democratic process. A report from the Horn of Africa put Eritrea on record as the one African nation that holds no elections. In the 2011 general elections in Liberia, former warlord Prince Yormie Johnson cruised the countryside wearing a red fez. The veteran fighter was seen winding down a window of his Ford Expedition as he tossed banknotes at assembled voters and then speed off to the next village or town. At one campaign event Mr. Johnson lambasted the sitting Liberian president for corruption, while one of his aides fretted about running out of cash to pay off journalists for good coverage.

This is the nature of African politics, not necessarily predicated on substance or issues but on need and popularity. Prince Johnson is one of the candidates who is biting for the second time in the 2017 presidential elections, as his popularity continues to rise in Liberia. African elections do not necessarily produce representative government, according to experts. In oil-rich but poverty-ridden Equatorial Guinea, President Teodoro Obiang was elected with 95 percent of the vote in 2009. His party also won 99 percent of the parliamentary seats. President Obiang has been in power since 1979, making him one of the longest-serving presidents in Africa. A look at Gambia, one of the smallest nations in Africa, shows that opposition parties in that West African nation have had less trust that its elections will be held on an equal plain. Rigging elections across the continent in Africa is nothing new, making experts to wonder if Western style democracy can truly be sustained. According to academic studies, there is a gloomy picture on the nature of democratic reform in most African countries. The annual democracy index of Economic Intelligent Units ranks Mauritius as the only African nation that is a "full" democracy.

The index uses tough criteria that count countries like much-praised Botswana as a "flawed democracy," a narrative that is open for debate given Botswana's impeccable record on democratic reform. According to the Mo Ibrahim Index, a quantitative measure of good governance, African political participation has seen a 5 percent decline since 2007. Another study by the Freedom House, an American think tank, reports that the number of full electoral democracy out of the forty-nine sub-Saharan African nations has dramatically declined, from 24 in 2005 to 19 at present. Even southern Africa, which has historically been considered the best performing region, is now a "problem child" according to this study. There is a record of nepotism and corruption in South Africa, the regional giant in southern Africa. In neighboring Madagascar, President Andre Rajoelina maintained power for three years after a bloodless coup.

In 2014, fifty-five-year-old Hery Rajaonarimampianina became Madagascar's president with the backing of the former president. Mr. Rajaonarimampianina is considered Madagascar's hope for economic change. In the same region, President Binguwa Mutharika of Malawi is behaving more despotically, behavior that has provoked Western donors to suspend their aid programs in the country. But in 2012, Malawi became the second African nation to put a female in the top leadership position of president after the death of President Binguwa Mutharika. In Angola, President Jose Eduardo Dos Santos has ruled the country since 1979, making him the longest-serving president in Africa. The cup is truly half full when one takes an inventory of democratic processes across the continent, giving some countries a thumb up, while other are above average. Yet some countries are struggling to make reform a priority.

It is fair to assert that Africa has come a long way from its colonial past toward self-determination. In 1990 the Freedom House did a study, indicating only three African countries had multiparty political systems, universal suffrage, regular fraud-free elections, and secret ballots. Since that time democratic progress has come in waves, according to Alex Vines, head of the African program at Chatham House, a London-based think tank. With the exception of Mali, the rest of West Africa has enjoyed a democratic boom. For example, Liberia and Sierra Leone, two nations that not too long ago came from violent backgrounds, have set up reputable if imperfect political systems; Guinea and Ivory Coast also overcame spasms of strife and now have returned to democratic rule. The nation of Guinea-Bissau recently held a calm election, while Nigeria and Niger ran their best polls in recent history.

Highly praised by President Barack Obama is Ghanaian democratic reform, West Africa's success story. The contrast is also clear, as election violence has become more common in a number of African nations. The DRC, Ivory Coast, Kenya, Nigeria, and Zimbabwe have seen serious clashes following the results of their most recent elections. Most election-related violence is sometimes caused by a long-standing ethnic and religious difference. Unlike previous decades of civil wars across the continent, these unrests are now more or less coming to swift ends. Progress in politics in the next decade may be a bite slower than in the past, but it is undeniable that many post-Cold War advances have been made. Those interested in reforms must realize that building firm institutions is harder than putting ballots in a box in Africa. However, there are lots of reasons for reformers to be hopeful as opposition parties and civil societies become sophisticated and gain resources. This new development in African politics is moving away from what used to be a mess in the past, undemocratic with few resources.

One observer described it as "the skunks at the democratic zoo," (*African Democracy*, 2012). Many people are still without hope about the political process in Africa, but some have learned that discipline and commitment can put things within striking distance of power. A few recent examples are political developments in Zambia and Senegal. One of the useful elements is the fact that voters are swayed by evidence of individual competence, not party affiliation, which tends to benefit opposition members who are competing with complacent governments. Due to Africa's high birth rates, a pool of young voters is more likely to take a chance on political newcomers entering into politics. In many African countries, a sitting president or party can win office with the support of a young population under thirty, as long as the process is fair. In 2006, football (soccer) superstar George Weah nearly won the presidential elections in Liberia with support from a population under thirty. Like Prince Johnson, Weah is also running for a second time in the upcoming presidential elections in 2017.

The rise of technology has improved communication in many African countries. Political campaigns no long need to depend on government-owned media or the ability to travel long distance. Voters can be reached directly and remotely through the Internet and mobile phones. Technology has made it easier to expose mismanagement and tabulate poll results instantly, making it easier to detect fraud during elections. In 2011, Nigeria's election was managed through the media; tens of thousands of monitors recorded local results and fed them by text messages into a central system run by volunteers. Research has shown that elections are one of the most-costly events in Africa. Lack of consistent and accurate voter data is another obstacle. Research also shows that most Africans, especially in rural areas, have no identity documents; as a result, electoral rolls often need to be drafted from scratch for every pool.

One of the most-costly elections was the 2011 election in the Democratic Republic of Congo (DRC). The government spent $500 million, making the DRC's elections the world's most-costly elections after the United States. Other obstacles in the electoral process are high rates of illiteracy and lack of capable help. In the border regions of Sierra Leone, election officials judge who should get a voting card by listening to people's accents to be sure they are not from Guinea or Liberia. Despite the quality of the democratic process in Africa, research shows that all but a few of the billion people on the continent now expect to vote in regular national polls. This is good news for Africa, compared to what 1.5 billion Asians, with all their impressive economic performance, cannot do.

Below is a classification of African countries according to level of civil service rehabilitation efforts, democratic reform and good governance:

A. **Full Democracy (Advance Reformers)**
   Seychelles
   Cape Verde Islands
   Botswana
   Mauritius
   Ghana
   South Africa

B. **Flawed Democracy (Committed Reformers)**
   Tunisia
   Tanzania
   Namibia
   Nigeria
   Benin
   Senegal
   Burkina Faso
   Rwanda
   Ethiopia
   Sierra Leone
   Kenya
   Zambia

C. **Hybrid Regimes (Hesitant Reformers)**
   Cote d'Ivoire (Ivory Coast)
   Gabon
   Guinea (Konakry)
   Niger
   Mali
   Uganda
   Togo
   Mozambique
   Egypt
   Malawi
   Mauritania

Morocco
Libya

D. Beginners and Nonstarters (Vicious Circle)
Congo
Burundi
Central African Republic
South Sudan
Swaziland
Cameroon
Somalia
Liberia
Somaliland

E. Authoritarian Regimes
Algeria
Zimbabwe
Sudan
Eritrea
Congo (Brazzaville)
The Democratic Republic of Congo (DRC)
Djibouti
Madagascar
Comoros Islands
Chad
Angola
Gabon
Cameroon
Guinea-Bissau

Sharing information among the reforming African countries is very vital to ensure sustainable improvement in African public administration systems. The idea is similar to the information-sharing policies among most Western countries, especially in the United States, regarding interstate commerce, law enforcement activities, and other important information between states. African countries with weak public services can improve their systems by following the footprints of the advanced-reforming or committed-reforming countries. Reinventing African public service by implementing homegrown methods is a major development, but it must be combined with the support of ethical and accountable changes in African countries in the "vicious circle" as a first step, according to experts. The attempt by public service ministers to work at reinventing the public administration must accept advance-reforming countries like Botswana, Namibia, South Africa, or Mauritius as focus points of orientation. It is true that foreign investments in African governments must not repeat the mistakes of the 1980s by letting donor countries pressure the implementation of reform schedules. The homegrown methods also offer some cultural advantages that encourage the involvement of African professionals with knowledge and expertise in doing business the African way. African professionals will understand the social dynamic of people and their needs.

DEMOCRATIC REFORM IN MAURITIUS

Overview

The republic of Mauritius is a group of islands in the southwest Indian Ocean, consisting of the main islands of Mauritius and Rodrigues, plus several outer islands. The islands of Mauritius and Rodrigues, with a total of 1, 969 square kilometers, have a total population density of 644 per square kilometer. The population is estimated at 1.3 million, comprising Hindus, Muslims, Sino-Mauritians, and those of mixed European and African origins (Singh, 2012). The nation of Mauritius has been successively a Dutch, French, and British colony. It became independent from Great Britain on March 12, 1968, and subsequently acceded to the status of republic within the Commonwealth on March 12, 1992. The official language of business is English, but French is widely spoken. Locally, however, Creole is the most predominant mother tongue, and ancestral languages are still spoken (EISA, 2005).

REFORM IN MAURITIUS: AFRICA'S SUCCESS STORY

Since independence in 1968, Mauritius has successfully transformed itself from a low-income, mono-crop agricultural economy based largely on sugarcane to an upper-middle-income country with a gross national income (GNI) per capita of US$8, 570 in 2012. The economic growth has been accompanied by significant progress in the areas of human development, good governance, and economic freedom. Mauritius has remained resilient in the wake of the world economic crisis. Due to a progressive implementation of a bold reform agenda, it has transitioned from a culture of administration to a focus on performance in the public sector. Mauritius has a good track record in respecting human and fundamental rights, as well as democratic principles, since its independence. When it comes to formulating public policy, the civil society and stakeholders are regularly consulted and involved in issues of national interest (National Assessment Report, 2010).

The country has a parliamentary democracy based on the Westminster system, a democratic parliamentary system of government modeled after the politics of the United Kingdom. In 2002, an important political development occurred in Mauritius when the island of Rodrigues obtained a significant autonomy, as well as its own regional assembly. In Mauritius, national and regional elections are held every five years under the universal adult franchise. According to that system, all registered electorates who have attained the eighteenth year have the right to vote. Mauritius is considered one of Africa's success stories. It is one of the most stable and democratic countries in Africa. Mauritius has an acceptable constitutional and legal framework; a largely satisfactory electoral system; a sound and transparent electoral process, and legitimate and credible electoral management bodies (Singh, 2012).

Freedom of speech, press, and assembly are protected, and the government generally respects these rights in practice. Mauritius is the first country in Africa that passed the post-block vote (FPTP-BV) and best-loser system. The advantage of the block vote system, according to experts, is that it allows voters preference for individual candidate. But it also has a disadvantage; if voters cast all their votes for candidates from the same party, the BV system produces highly disproportional results. As the record shows, Mauritius has one of the best democratic systems on the continent. One of the most prevalent issues that produces conflicts in Africa is lack of a free and fair election. Mauritius has been very fortunate, holding elections for more than forty years without falling victim to serious electoral conflict. This is the reason why Mauritius is considered one of the most stable and democratic countries in Africa. As a result, its citizens enjoy political and civil rights.

This does not mean the country has no challenges, especially when it comes to elections. Any electoral challenges are managed through the judicial process. The government is committed to upholding the fundamental principles of human rights and freedom embodied in its constitution. It also upholds the legal framework in holding free, fair, and credible elections. A practice that is prohibited in Mauritius's electoral process is vote buying or forcing citizens to vote against their will, which are very common in most African and many developing countries. Reports show that no vote-buying incident has been found so far in this tiny island nation. In an effort to prevent such a flaw, all the electorates have mobile phone to inform police officials if there are any concerns. The use of mobiles, especially on the eve of elections, is very strong to ensure free and fair elections in Mauritius. The media is a critical stakeholder in helping the electorate to make a well-informed choice. In order to influence voters, prospective candidates use newspaper, radio, and TV stations.

UNDP's Support for Reform in Mauritius

With the support of the United Nations Development Program (UNDP), Mauritius has put in a budget management process through the introduction of the Program-Based Budgeting (PBB) system. In 2007, UNDP introduced the PBB system to improve transparency and accountability. The program was recognized by the collaborative African Budget Institute (CABRI) as the "big bang" because rolled out to all the ministries' land departments simultaneously rather than being piloted in selected institutions.

The PBB system is an integrated approach that has changed the focus of the Mauritian budgetary process from an input-based annual activity to a performance-based exercise with a key objective: to improve expenditure efficiency and effectiveness by systematically linking funding to results through the use of performance information (UNDP, 2013). The aim of the PBB program is to allocate public resources in line with the government's priorities and improve the performance orientation of the budget process.

In order to ensure success, the PBB reform continues to receive technical support from UNDP. Since the introduction of program-based budgeting, the Mauritian government has put in place a budget management process by linking public resources to clear and agreed outcomes and outputs. The process provides a framework for reporting on results and has encouraged stronger performance accountability. Under the UNDP's leadership and guidance, all government ministries are required to prepare a three-year PBB strategic plan for the first time since 2011.

An evaluation of public finance management showed significant progress in comparison to previous projects. Mauritius has received international recognition for its budget reforms. As a result, several African countries have requested that Mauritius share its experience with them. In 2013, a study tour on the PBB reform was organized; participating were three delegations of senior budget officials from Maldives, Zanzibar, and Burkina Faso.

Another area that UNDP supports in Mauritius is human resources management to further strengthen the PBB approach. An important parallel is in the area of investment project planning (IPP). The IPP project enabled the Mauritian government to identify successful investment projects in line with longer-term strategic directions for Mauritius in the following ways:

- Set up the Project Planning Committee, an Inter-Ministerial committee mandated to assess project proposals before they are considered for the budget
- Investment in staff training and development efforts
- Development of the Investment Project Process Manual, which defines the evaluation criteria for a new project

In 2012, the Mauritian government decided on an initiative to formulate a ten-year national plan known as the Economic and Social Transformation Plan (ESTP). The ESTP, according to the Mauritian government, is expected to enhance the benefits of PBB by integrating the three-year budget into a long-term prospectus. Experts believe the ESTP will establish the road map to the country's future and provide the physical infrastructure and human resources to support progress and development. It will also accelerate pace in a sustainable and equitable way and move Mauritius from an upper-income country to a high-income country (GNI of $12, 615 per capita) by 2022.

The ESTP initiative is intended to generate significant economic growth in Mauritius. The final project UNDP is supporting in Mauritius is the Learning Management System (LMS) which was tailor-made for the Mauritian civil service through an e-learning platform. UNDP supported setting up the LNS, writing and designing a first course on basic public finance management (PFM). The agency is assisting with setting up a web-based interface with the goal of making the first PFM course accessible to ten thousand civil servants.

Some illustrations of Mauritius's success have to do with the government's ability to cooperate and collaborate with the international communities with the view to work for the benefit of the population and meeting the objectives of the international organizations. An example is Mauritius's willingness to combat terrorism at the beginning of the millennium by passing the Terrorism Act in 2002. The government also supports the international community's fight against piracy, which was causing much harm in the Indian Ocean.

When it comes to internal management of the society, the Mauritian government has tried its level best to practice good governance by allowing the population the opportunity to voice their opinions and views. That is the true meaning of good governance; it refers to the process of decision making and the process by which decisions are implemented or not implemented (Suntoo, 2012). The UNDP defines *good governance* as the exercise of political, economic, and administrative authority to manage a nation's affairs. Cleary and McConville (2006) argued that good governance occurs when the state, free of abuse and corruption, conducts and manages public affairs and public resources efficiently and effectively.

They assert that good government means doing the right thing in the right way with due regard to the law. According to the United Nations Commission, there are eight principles and practices of good governance: participation, rule of law, transparency, responsiveness, equity and inclusiveness, consensus orientation, effectiveness and efficiency, and accountability. A close look at Mauritius' governance record reveals that most of the principles are carefully observed. But it is also fair to argue that there is always room for improvement in any modern democracy. In any nation (developed or under developed), there are issues to deal with. [1]

GHANA: AFRICA'S SUCCESS STORY OF GOOD GOVERNANCE

A few countries in Africa are considered success stories when it comes good governance, despite the challenges with accountability many still face. One of those nations is Ghana, which, due to its aggressive agenda of reform, has continued to enjoy a robust economy. Ghana, like many other African countries, experienced a great expansion in the civil service sector after the 1960s. The global oil crisis during that time period meant an African economic decline, ending the ideal of business-oriented reforms of public administration, which had brought growth (Adamolekum 2005, p.1). As a remedy to the crisis, donor countries provided African states with the necessary financial assistance to make up for the cutbacks in civil service, in the case of Ghana to enhance accessibility. The shrinking of the Ghanaian public administration was tackled through several reform steps. Among the steps taken was a grand movement of organizational restructuring that led to a reorganization of the government ministries. The reform efforts resulted in the elimination of four unnecessary agencies during that time period. The other method, which was very well supported by the donor countries, was the Ghanaian retrenchment policy. Donor

---

[1] Detail of good governance and democratic process in Amamolekum's 2005 account of what's working in Ghana and the current status of democracy.

countries favored the approach due to the conviction that a smaller public sector would work more efficiently, given the UK's experience, for instance (Chaudhry 1993, p. 246).

Another development that received much support from donor countries was the idea of a rollback of the state. The involvement of the state was seen as one of the major problems in developing countries after the 1970s. The primary goal of the policy was to cut back unneeded civil servants in order to shrink the country's public administration system, reducing the number of civil servants from 131, 089 in 1990 to 80,000 in 1995 (Olowu 1999, p. 4–5). Despite the reduction of Ghanaian civil servants, their pay was increased, decomposing the wages and providing higher salaries for public managers. Interestingly, the information about the increases varies depending on the source. The actual salaries in Ghana, according to experts, did not rise significantly. Although salaries were much higher than in many African countries, the increase during the reform period was modest. According to experts, the retrenchment of Ghanaian civil servants in general proved to be more-costly than expected in the beginning.

Despite the cumulative losses as a result of downsizing in the 1980s, Ghana is classified as a committed reformer. The Ghanaian reform program can find its place in history without criticism from Robert Dodoo, former head of the Ghanaian civil servants, who asserted his dissatisfaction in regard to the reform movement. According to him, the fundamental reason for the lack of improvement in the country's development lay in the "donor time-table, agendas and conditionality" (Dodoo, 1996, p. 30).

While it is true the external financial support was necessary and vital for improvement of the Ghanaian civil service, the provision of money came with unreasonable short-term expectations. It does not seem surprising that a country in danger of losing all monetary support decides to hustle through a reform and risk less successful implementation policies instead of losing crucial financial aid. Research identified two core weaknesses after the evaluation of the first part of the Ghanaian service reform:

1. The manner in which reform was embarked upon
2. The overall goal of the reform

As indicated by Mr. Dodoo, the pressure for success coming from donor countries was not beneficial for the improvement of the Ghanaian civil service. Ghana, like many African nations that received external financial support, had agreed to reduce the cost of the public sector and implement some questionable structural adjustments in its programs as a condition for financial support from the International Monetary Fund and the World Bank. The results of such cost savings were modest. The question is why reduce the African public administration to begin with? The African civil service was no bigger than those in many other states. Expanding it after the colonial rulers granted independence was a vital step toward a functioning economy and sustainable development for countries like Ghana.

Even the World Bank agrees in the following policy statement: "An effective state is vital for the provision of goods and services—and the rules and institutions—that allow markets to flourish and people to lead wealthier, happier lives. Without sustainable development, both economic and social advancement are impossible" (World Bank, 1997). The third reform step that was evaluated was the alteration of salaries in the civil service. While there was some increase in the salaries of civil servants in Ghana, studies show that they were relatively low, especially since highly qualified human capital will usually leave the country for better-paid jobs. Often, high-qualified human capital will leave and travel to Western countries for better-paid jobs or become open to corruption. The problem of corruption is another major weakness of African public administration, added to practices such as nepotism, sectionalism, and tribalism. A study by the IMF shows a strong correlation between wages in public administration relative to wages in manufacturing: "It is estimated that government wages needed to be 2x8 (...) times higher to make corruption negligible." The other repercussions of corruption in Africa are the waste of financial resources and cancelation of international aid programs as punishment.

IMPROVEMENT

To reinvent a successful policy of African public administration, public service ministers came together in Stellenbosch, South Africa, in 2003 to respond to the "unfolding challenges." The goal of the new reform is to switch to homegrown and demand-driven methods directed at specific problems and challenges instead of the goals of broad downsizing and cost-cutting policies as donors demanded. Another argument has to do with ethics in public management, which has a fundamental influence in the quality of decisions made in public administration, as Von Maravic argues (Maravic 2009, p. 3). If one could ensure the ethical comportment of African public officials, public administration could be highly improved. Another problem that faces African public administration is lack of resources. According to the United Nations, "In many countries around the world, but in African countries in particular, public administration remains weak largely owing to a shortage of human resources and deficiencies in staff training and motivation" (UN, 2005, p. 13). One has to be cautious not to apply improving African public service reform to all African countries. There is a significant differentiation that provides a possible classification of African countries that must be taken to account when referring to Ghana as a reform-committed country.

Ghana has made significant democratic gains since it made a transition from a quasi-military to a democratic government in 1992. In spite of major challenges that still exist, the nation has not suffered any economic stagnation or gone back to an unstable democracy, as has occurred in other African countries. The strength of the Ghanaian democracy was recently put to test following the death of President John Evans Atta Mills in July 2012, with the smooth transfer of the power of government to the vice president. The peaceful transition was an indication of how far Ghanaian democracy has come. Ghana has seen continuous improvement in the competitiveness, peacefulness, and credibility of its multiparty elections as demonstrated by the two peaceful turnovers of the executive power following the 2008 and 2012 presidential elections. When it comes to the transition to democracy, the Ghanaian parliament inherited a very weak institutional structure due to the fact that preceding military governments had no role to play. According to studies on Ghanaian democracy, the executive had significant representation in the parliament and a strong whip system, which allows a vast patronage powers to the incumbent president. As a result, the executive branch of government largely succeeds in getting its policies through the House. The reform policy has to look at the interpretation of article 108 of the Ghanaian constitution to prevent the parliament from proposing any initiative or bill that places a financial burden on the state. As difficult as these challenges were, the reform process had to deal with them to bring about the level of transparency and accountability that has made Ghana one of the committed reformers in Africa.

THE IMPACT OF FOREIGN AID ON GHANAIAN DEMOCRACY

Assistance from donors has helped to support and promote elections, Ghanaian parliamentary reforms, political parties, civil society, and the role of media in Ghana. While it is fair to argue that aid from donors has made a tremendous difference, it still faces some obstacles to promote further democratic process in Ghana. The recent growth of budget support, which plays a positive role in promoting Ghana's ownership of its own development process, has a practical effect on the marginalization of parliament's role in financial affairs. According to experts, many budgetary decisions that have to do with how budget support is accepted and how it is used are made by the president and the finance ministry and are subject to only perfunctory approval by parliament. Donors have continued to support the civil society organizations. That effort has enabled civil society organizations to undertake a number of successful projects locally to increase governmental transparency and accountability. An example is the financing of the 1996 project, spearheaded by local civic groups, to carry out the first nonpartisan election observation. Another donor-funded project in 2000 enabled civic groups to observe and report on the unfair treatment and inadequate coverage of opposition parties in the media. That project made a significant difference in addressing concern of electoral fairness in Ghana.

Donors have also helped to promote a fruitful dialogue between parties concerning issues of election fraud. One of those interventions was the creation of the Inter-Party Advisory Committee (IPAC) in1995, funded by donors. As a result of IPAC, opposition parties won concessions that led to several transparencies to enhance reforms at election time. The policy enables counting at polling stations, transparency of ballot boxes, and permission given to party agents to be present at polling stations. The Advisory Committee helped to restore trust in the electoral process by the opposition, as well as greatly contributing to the competitiveness and credibility of the 1996 elections compared to the previous one. Due to Ghana's history of executive dominance, donors were allowed to provide the most extensive support in strengthening the parliament's capacity to oversee the country's financial affairs by running training workshops and exchanging visits, as well as providing support for a number of parliamentary committees, especially the public accounts committee (Gyimah et al, 2012).

BOTSWANA: A MIRACLE IN AFRICAN DEMOCRACY

In November 2008, the former president of Botswana, Festus Gontebanye Mogae, was honored with the Ibrahim Prize for Achievement in African Leadership. The Mo Ibrahim Foundation awards the prize to a former African head of state who was democratically elected and served within the term limits set by the country's constitution. The foundation did an assessment of sub-Saharan leaders in their exercise of good leadership and the country's performance during their term of office. The award is one of the largest annual awards in the world and consists of $5 million over ten years and $200, 000 annually thereafter for life. President Mogae also won an additional $200,000-per-year grant for ten years for leaders who take on public interest activities and espouse good causes. According to research, the international community has long considered Botswana a success story on the African continent.

Since its independence in 1966, it has maintained high economic growth, sound fiscal policies, and regular elections. For Botswana, like most African nations with a record of economic growth and political stability, such a label of success tends to outweigh the need to ensure proper compliance with international human rights laws. In the case of Botswana, in spite of the success story, there is inequality, discrimination, and a dominant single political party. One of those human rights issues is the long and complicated relationship between the San (also known as the Bushmen, or Basarwa) and the ruling elite, who mostly come from the Tswana ethic group. The ethnic division has led to the San's vulnerable position in Botswana society under the name "Batswana" as opposed "Botswana," which is used to refer to the people of Botswana.

Another example of the complicated relationship is the eviction of the ethnic San Bushmen from their homeland in the central Kalahari Game Reserve by the government of Botswana, presumably to make way for exploration for diamond mines. This controversy over land rights between the government and the San is considered the longest and most expensive court cases in the history of the country. Throughout Africa, whether in good economic and politically stable climates or not, ethnic tension between groups is very common. The country also faces other challenges, such as the HIV/AIDS pandemic that threatens the future of the country and people, combating corruption, and ensuring an environment conducive to peace, security, and development based on the rule of law and respect for human rights. Botswana has managed to address each of these challenges in a balanced way.

Many experts have argued that economic growth and political stability lead to advancement in human rights, according to a competitive analysis of democratic development in African nations like Tunisia, Botswana, and Ghana (Tiruneh, 2004). The advancement of human rights is fundamentally dependent on the creation of a stable and thriving democracy. Economic growth can lead to improvement in the education system, the pillar to sustain a modern democracy. When one considers the state of affairs in many African countries, these basic improvements in quality of life remain major challenges. The role then for civil society is to engage the state to demonstrate a leadership that will ensure such policy. Civil society can collaborate with African governments to formulate policies that address these basic human rights issues.

Once the livelihood is improved, political stability is guaranteed. The claim that Botswana is the "Miracle of Africa" is clearly put into prospective because the country has enjoyed economic growth and political stability for many decades since the period of its independence in 1966. In this context, scholars have made the argument that Botswana's success in achieving such economic prosperity and political stability means it is one of Africa's most committed reform nations.

REASON FOR BOTSWANA'S PROSPERITY

According to studies (Acemoglu et al., "An African Success Story," 2001), there are reasons for Botswana's post-protectorate success. The studies show several reasons for the success, including the country's unique history and context; a few are coincidental, and some are the byproduct of efforts by the country's leaders. Experts and leaders, like former president of Botswana Quett Masire and scholars including Abdi Samatar, Daron Acemoglu, Simon Johnson, James A. Robinson, J. Clark Leith, and Stephen Lewis, all applaud Botswana as "the African Miracle" because of the country's political stability, regular elections, consistent economic growth, and sound investment policies. Following the discovery of significant diamond reserves, the government of Botswana pursued sound fiscal policies to ensure that the country's diamond wealth was not squandered.

The government increased its investments through "responsibly handled dealings with foreign corporations and management of the state enterprises" (Olmstewad, 2004, p.799, 801). The leadership of the nation made a decision to ensure that it utilized the wealth afforded by its natural resources wisely, which allowed them to accomplish great economic feats. As a consequence, since its independence Botswana has maintained one of the strongest GDP growth rates not only in Africa but in the world. According to UNICEF, Botswana's GDP growth rates between 1970 through 1999 averaged 8.3 percent.

CAPE VERDE

Overview

The islands of Cape Verde, a former Portuguese colony, stand out as one of Africa's exceptional nations. Achieving independence in 1975, Cape Verde shared a unique feature with Guinea-Bissau, another former Portuguese colony also located on the west coast of Africa. Both Cape Verde and Guinea-Bissau had the same liberation movement, known as the African Party for the Independence of Guinea-Bissau and Cape Verde (PAIGC). The movement took power from the colonial administration. Eventually, the two nations took dramatically different paths after a coup d'état in Guinea-Bissau in 1980 with the formation of PAICV, a Cape Verdean wing of the PAIGC. Portugal, the former colonial power, had employed Cape Verdeans in its colonial administration in Guinea-Bissau, where the independence movement was launched. Studies indicated that some Cape Verdeans were involved in the core group during the independence movement in Guinea-Bissau (Meyns, 2002).

The two nations also shared social and cultural connections, given their colonial history. The founding father of the movement, Amilcar Cabral, whom the Amilcar Cabral Estate in Monrovia, Liberia, was named in honor of, was born in Guinea-Bissau of Cape Verdean parents. Cabral was the prime architect of the concept of unity for Guinea-Bissau and the Cape Verde Islands. His idea was to unite both countries in order to achieve independence. The concern was that it would be difficult to conduct an anticolonial struggle on the islands of Cape Verde for fear that Portugal will likely draw them close to its fold. Looking back now, one can see that Cabral's concept of unity, an expression of strategic thinking, clearly served its purpose during the liberation struggle in the early history of Cape Verde and Guinea-Bissau.

A SUCCESS CASE OF POLITICAL REFORM

Cape Verde's success story put her in the ranks of the few other African countries that have experienced a renewed change of government. Examples of countries achieving successful elections include Benin and Sao Tomé and Principe. In the past decades, other African countries have also recorded notable reforms and democratic transformations, including Ghana, Senegal, and Mauritius, where this level of political reform has occurred more often than anywhere else in Africa. Comparatively, in the last two decades, countries such as Botswana and South Africa have also enjoyed sustained electoral dominance by a single party and still maintained democratic conciliation. Although peace and stability have been the bottom line in these situations, the worldwide experience usually ends in extended rule by a single party, despite the legitimate election results. A typical example of single-party rule is Liberia, where the True

Whig Party was in control of politics for 130 years. The problem in these circumstances, more often than not, is that they undermined the ideas of accountability and transparency.

What sets these African countries apart from those that are not considered Africa's success stories? Major differences include respect for the rule of law and fair democratic competition among the ruling party and opposition parties. Other differentiators are stability and free and fair electoral processes, without major intimidation of citizens. These variables experts consider central to making these countries exemplary. What makes the comparative success of Cape Verde's democratic development additionally interesting, according to meta-analysis studies of the country, is that this island nation belongs to the group of African countries in which anticolonial liberation movements took over power after independence. Compared to other Portuguese colonies in Africa, Cape Verde achieved its independence only after protracted struggle, eventually overthrowing the corporatist regime in its formal capital, Lisbon, in 1974.

After its recent democratic transition, Cape Verde has been free of the violent upheavals that have thrown other African countries, like Angola and Mozambique, into disarray. This underscores the need to look at what makes each African country unique in its struggle for change. In the case of Cape Verde, its leaders made a decision to examine its structural and historical features as an island state in the Atlantic, its institutional set up, and the nature of the changes that began during the 1990–1991 period. The history and structure of the country and the social dynamic of the people were the underlining causes for accomplishing its national objectives. When a state perceives a need that impacts its citizens, the efforts to do something about such needs becomes a national priority. In the case of Cape Verde, democratic reform was a national priority. Cape Verde also had a much lesser challenge in obtaining self-governance because more of the process of political mobilization took place in Guinea-Bissau. Cape Verde had a commercial economy as opposed to Guinea-Bissau, which had a subsistence-based economy (Lobban, 1996).

Cape Verde has also made a number of reforms by carrying out ambitious foreign policy decisions, such as its good neighbors in fishing and maritime agreement, as well as new friends around the world and a positive role at the United Nations Security Council in matters from Rwanda refugees to Angolan elections. The country has invested in several development initiatives, like infrastructure improvements, including roads, ports, power, and water; expansion of tourism, and very liberal investment plans without taxes or profit repatriation. The island nation has improved its telecommunications, air transport, and fishing industries. Although much has been accomplished in reforming the democratic process, the ruling party must do more to regain the confidence of the people, especially the opposition party, where there is a need to weather criticism. More remarkable is the bloodless political transition to full-scale plural democracy. The Cape Verdean democracy can serve as a model to those African nations that wish to move from one-party rule to political pluralism and from military rule to secular democratic societies. An example is the new maritime border treaty between Guinea-Bissau and Guinea-Conakry, which was signed without conflict.

SEYCHELLES: A PARABLE OF SUCCESS

Overview

This 115-island nation located four degrees south of the equator in the western Indian Ocean has been one of Africa's success stories. The islands are scattered over 150,000 square miles of the Indian Ocean, a thousand miles east of the coast of Kenya. Like the Galapagos Islands in South America, the Seychelles (commonly pronounced *Say-shells*) is inhabited by 850 species of fish, 100 kinds of shellfish, and many animals and plant species that are found nowhere else on the continent of Africa. The islands are all that remain after the African and Indian continents separated millions of years ago. According to geologists, the major islands consist of pre-Cambrian granite over 650 million years old, not the fossilized coral the forms most of the Caribbean islands (O'Keefe, 1988). The people of Seychelles are a mixture of Indians, Europeans, Asians, and Africans. Three languages are officially taught in school: English, French, and Creole. However, Creole is the common language used in the country marketplaces.

Although the islands are four degrees from the equator, the people of Seychelles do experience changes in seasons primarily marked by the monsoon winds, a weather type that also affects countries in Southeast Asia, including India, Malaysia, Thailand, the Philippines, Burma, and Vietnam. From the months of May to November, the monsoons (also known as the trade winds) come from Southeast Asia, and prolonged heavy rainfall is infrequent. In the months of December and January, much of the ninety-three inches of annual rainfall usually pours from the skies, sometimes reaching up to three inches an hour. The islands were first inhabited in the 17th century, but they remain much as they were thousands of years ago. The islands are beautiful and awesome; no one who gazes upon the granite cliffs where tropical birds soar can fail to sense the timeless lineage that speaks to its rich naturalness. The population of Seychelles islands as of 2015 is estimated to be 92,000, placing the islands at 195 in the world.

The island of Mahé (of mixed African-European and Indian heritage) is the largest of the islands and where the sleepy little capital city of Victoria is located. Victoria, named after England's Queen Victoria, is the most populated city in Seychelles, with a population of 65,000. Victoria is 27 km (miles) long and 7 km (miles) wide. Its mountainous green suburbs are inhabited by over 30,000 people. Seychelles is one of the most delightful places to live in Africa, full of some of the most beautiful people on the continent (p. 44). Tourists are most attracted by its pure blue ocean along the shores of the coastline. There are many habitats in some of the smaller islands, adding to the natural riches of the island nation. Like most African countries, Seychelles has not always been a success story; there was a coup in June 1977 that overthrew the first executive president. Other issues include class and racial divisions, poverty, and shantytowns, which pose a major challenge for the current government.

A PARABLE OF SUCCESS

In an interview with *New African,* James Michel, president of Seychelles, responded to a question about how they did it: "We accepted our own mistakes, abandoned what was not working, and embraced reform by putting the interests of the country first above any political considerations. That way we gave hope to the people that they can enjoy a more prosperous future" (Kabukuru, 2014). The president's response demonstrates what's working in Africa. The parable of the success story in Seychelles began in 2008 when the government initiated a wide platform of economic reforms in this Indian Ocean island nation. Economic reform was one of the most difficult initiatives ever taken since the country's independence in 1976, according to President Michel. The economic model of Seychelles was characterized by heavy state intervention in the economy. It was a well-spread welfare system unmatched in Africa; surpassing or equaling the European welfare platform.

In an attempt to change the country's socialist-leaning economic direction at a time when Seychelles was on the verge of economic difficulties, the president took an unpleasant path that most in the country initially disagreed with. This is what transformative leaders do, changing the directions of a nation and raising people's hopes. Sometimes such decisions are not always popular at the beginning. The ideas were also intended to release Seychelles, already overburdened by debt and imbalance in international repayments. Repayment of debt is one of the issues that continue to be major obstacles in many African nations that are trying to reform their economies. The government decided to overhaul the country's fiscal policies and liberated the economy by reducing state monopolies and controls. Another factor in the success was opening up state enterprises for privatization, along with reforms of the civil service; all contributed to a complete redefinition of the economy.

Although Seychelles has very few natural resources, it has a GDP per capita of US$8,000, the highest in Africa. Next to Seychelles in high GDP per capita is Mauritius, with US$2,000 (*New African*, 2014). Seychelles also has a literacy rate of 95 percent, due to its free education policy, and a health care system that works. It has one of the most robust housing policies in Africa. Eleven thousands of the twenty-five thousand housing units in the country were built by the government for poor people at a very low cost. The average person in Seychelles today is living better than he or she was in 1977 during the liberation. The government's investment in education and health care has placed the country in the highest development ranking in Africa. According to the current Human Development Index, Seychelles is ranked forty-seventh out of 177 countries, the highest in Africa. The island nation enjoys the continent's highest life expectancy rates at 72 (male: 66.69 and female: 77.63 years) and the lowest infant mortality rates on the continent.

ELECTORAL PROCESS

Seychelles uses a mixed electoral system that allows twenty-five members to be directly elected by a simple majority vote, according to its constitution. The remaining, at least one-half of the majority members, are chosen by proportional representation. In other words, it is an electoral system by which divisions in an electorate are reflected proportionately in the elected body. For example, if 30 percent of the electorate supports a particular political party, then roughly 30 percent of seats will be won by that party. Consequently, in Seychelles, any party that has polled an aggregate 10 percent or more of the total votes cast can nominate a proportionally elected member for each 10 percent of the votes polled. In 1992, a system was put in place that allows free referendum and elections to determine the will of the people. According to a *New African* report, 2006 was the seventh national poll since the return of the multiparty policies (p. 284). Transparency in the electoral system is one of the core principles of Seychelles' democratic efforts. If such reform works in Seychelles, it can also work anywhere in Africa. The question is, do leaders of other African nations have the political courage and the will? It takes commitment and dedication to bring about meaningful change. Sometimes such decisions are not always popular initially.

CHALLENGES

While it is true that Seychelles has made tremendous improvement in governance, education, and health care, there are challenges in areas such as Freedom House. Experts believed that President Michel is sincere when he says he wants social cohesion; however, this may only be possible if it is followed by opening up the political process further. The assumption is that such a move will be challenged by members of his own party many of whom have grown accustomed to a virtual monopoly of power and would not embrace such change, which might open the possibility of defeat. Part of the challenge is the life-long influence of former prime minister France René of the party. This would mean facing down the former prime minister and his supporters in the ruling party; which will mean a clear separation of the party from the government. It would also demonstrate a determined resistance to the old habits of undermining the democratic institutions through patronage and partisanship (Baker, 2008).

The former prime minister came to power in a bloodless coup that overthrew President James Mancham one year after independence. In 2004 René announced that he was resigning in favor of then Vice President James Michele but continued to have a solid influence in the ruling party. When it comes to democratic reform, much credit is given to President Michele, whose political courage and determination has led to major transformations in Seychelles. Visionary leaders usually see things that the rest of society does not see. President William Tolbert was one of those African leaders. Although Tolbert was president of Liberia for only nine years and served for ten months as chairman of the OAU, which is now the African Union (AU), his vision led to the creation of regional organization like West African Economic Community, the Mano River Union (MRU), and West Africa's Rice Development Association (WARDA), promoting true African unity. He also instituted a policy of Total Involvement for Higher Heights and humanist capitalism in Liberia.

CHAPTER SIX

COMMITTED REFORMERS OR FLAWED DEMOCRACY?

TUNISIA: THE ARAB SPRING'S PIVOTAL DEMOCRATIC SUCCESS STORY

In 2011 Tunisia confronted a long list of challenges to the creation of democratic reform. The expectations for swift and wide-ranging reforms were high among a population that was hungry for change after decades of harsh authoritarian rule. Ordinary Tunisians were eager to enjoy the benefits of meaningful political freedom and economic prosperity. The expectation followed a decade of enduring unrelenting repression and mismanagement and the plundering of resources by a small circle around the family of the country's former president Zine al-Abidine Ben Ali. The wake of the Arab Spring and the departure of the dictator took a toll on the Tunisian economy, its tourism industry in particular. About 500,000 people out of a population of 10 million depend on the tourism sector. The instability in neighboring Libya has had a negative effect on Tunisia's much-needed trade revenue.

With the difficult economic and social pressures, there is a sense among the Tunisian public that the reform effort may be too slow, making the population increasingly frustrated. Democracy advocates outside of

Tunisia are watching with concern; the country is considered a bellwether of the revolution that has engulfed the region. Although it is still early in Tunisia's post-Ben Ali regime, the country is approaching a very pivotal moment in its reform efforts that will require patience from its citizens. The success of the efforts for change will need meaningful support from the world's democratic institutions, such as the United States and the European Union, first and foremost. One of the major challenges facing the country is the shortage of food in some regions, which is threatening the social stability. Improving these issues will require keeping on track with the democratic process to ensure accountability and transparency of policy implementation. Part of the transparency and accountability efforts is having free and fair elections to sustain Tunisia's democratic development.

Tunisia, like most Arab nations have been, was a closed society for many decades that is now opening with remarkable speed. However, there are still impacts on its institutions and society after years of repression, corruption, and mismanagement. The country's political rights rating in Freedom in the World, based on Freedom House's annual assessment of political rights and civil liberties, was the same as those of Sudan and Chad in 2010. Its civil-liberties rating was no better, placing Tunisia alongside other repressive countries, such as Qatar, Tajikistan, and Vietnam. Tunisia's standing regarding freedom of the press, as analyzed by the freedom of print and broadcast media, was at the level of notoriously repressive regimes like Equatorial Guinea, Laos, and Syria. Out of the 196 countries covered in the assessment, Tunisia ranked 184th. That said, the system cannot be transformed overnight into transparent and accountable democratic governance.

The country has made much progress compared to its neighbors. However, there is a lot more to be done. Change is always difficult, especially institutional change, but there is great potential for gains in freedom of expression and assembly, according to experts. A number of reforms have taken place since the removal of the former president. For example, the news media are experiencing an openness unimaginable when Ben Ali was in power. Freedom of assembly, where citizens have repeatedly mounted demonstrations to air their grievances and demands, and the adoption of the new press code are some of the reform efforts that have gained support from the people (Walker and Tucker, 2011). A transparent election process will ensure public confidence and trust, as well as that of the international community.

The challenging starting point for Tunisia's reform efforts should serve as a reminder of the task it must undertake before the country can begin to meet its basic democratic principles. This challenge must be embraced by the international communities with vested interests in the region, such as the United States and the European Union, by providing appropriate support to sustain the reform efforts. Tunisia's example in carrying out this positive post-revolutionary role and institution building has had an impact on Egypt's democracy. It will eventually have an impact on other countries that are emerging from authoritarian regimes to hold free and fair elections on their own in North Africa. On the other hand, it would be a missed opportunity for the region and for the strategic interests of the United States and the European Union if Tunisia's reform efforts fail.

The European Union particularly should be more involved in supporting Tunisia's democratic transition efforts for historic, economic, and strategic reasons. European Union support for Tunisia's effort to build and reform its institutions and move toward a consolidated democracy will lead to a functioning market economy. Consolidating democracy, economic development, stability, and security at Europe's southern borders is necessary because that will ensure a stable and secure southern border. Secondly, economic growth is a necessary condition for consolidating democratic and political reforms in Tunisia and North Africa in general (Dandashly, 2012). Tunisia is the first successful case of a larger project that will include other North African countries, such as Morocco and Algeria.

Tunisia's case is unique because it has a strong statehood and a modern society with strong ties to the French system and culture. Compared to its neighbors, Tunisia has a highly educated, coherent population and an active civil society. The role of civil society cannot be underestimated in any democratic reform efforts, whether in Tunisia or elsewhere. Supporting the democratic process and building institutions in Tunisia is affordable to the European Union, according to experts. Such efforts will have positive spillovers to the rest of the region, demonstrating that democracy is affordable and can succeed in the Arab world.

ECONOMIC DEVELOPMENT IN TUNISIA

Swift actions to address the needs of the country are required for the democratic reform efforts to continue. Some of the needs to address are the increasingly high unemployment rate and low job growth, especially among the youth, due to the disproportion between the increase in educated and skilled youth and the tight domestic market, poverty, and social inequality. In order to more drastically change the situation, Tunisia is seeking EU's support to address the socioeconomic problems in the marginalized regions. Other institutions supporting Tunisian reform efforts are the World Bank and European Bank for Reconstruction and Development (EBRD), working in partnership with other international organizations and influential powers that have promised financial support to certain projects to attract investments, create more jobs, and increase growth (World Bank, 2012).

Based on consultations with the emerging civil society on the priorities of the Tunisian economy, the international community is working together to provide financial and technical assistance to support the government's efforts to create and implement reform programs that address the urgent economic needs. Creating an environment that is suitable to attract investments and facilitates the opening of businesses is critical to the government. The international community will not only provide financial support to target economic growth but also share its experience regarding democratization and reforms of the market economy. It is not enough to prepare plans and fund development projects. In order to have a prosperous economy, Tunisia, in partnership with the international community, needs to train the labor force and reform the educational system. An education that meets international standards is needed across the continent to have a competitive edge in the global economy.

THE ROLE OF CIVIL SOCIETY IN TUNISIA

The role civil society is always critical in any reform efforts, whether in Tunisia or other parts of Africa. Civil society serves as a watchdog for the functions of government. The concept of separation of power and the responsibility of the executive, legislative, and judiciary branches is critical when it comes to basic freedom and accountability. Those are the fundamental principles and values of democracy. The faster these reform efforts are implemented, the more the economic situation of the country will be improved. It is necessary for the Tunisian government to adopt all of its important institutional reforms to build a democratic system and a functional market economy.

One of the steps needed to achieve such a democratic system is to amend the constitution and reform the legal system in order to make it suitable for a new democratic system based on respect for human rights and civil liberties. The universal declaration of human rights principles also includes the principles of rule of law and gender equality at workplaces and in all aspects of social and political life. The universal principles are accountability, transparency, the freedom of expression, religion, and association, or assembly. The Tunisian government has accomplished much in a very short period; however, there is a lot more work to be done in the reform efforts. The good news is the country is heading in the right direction as a success story in North Africa and an example that the rest of North Africa and Arab world has been inspired by.

A LOOK AT DEMOCRACY IN TANZANIA

Overview

What is today known as Tanzania Mainland began with a transition from colonial rule to independence in 1961. The 1961 constitution provided an elected government, a parliamentary system, competitive multiparty politics, and a liberal democratic political and judicial process. But in 1962, a year after independence, the constitution was enacted, ushering in the presidential system, with the executive branch headed by the president as head of the state and the government. To pave the way for a strong executive power, another act was passed in 1963. The legislation was known as the Preventive Detention Act, which gave the president power to arrest and imprisons any person regarded to be a danger to the state, similar to the public relations officers during President Tubman's administration in Liberia, where certain individuals were responsible to report suspicious person(s) to the president.

On January 14, 1963, newly elected president Julius Kamarage Nyerere announced that Tanganyika would be a one-party state, arguing that the decision was in the interest of national unity and rapid economic development. Like postcolonial governments in Africa at the time, the idea of a one-party political system was common throughout Africa. In Tanganyika, the ruling party was the Tanganyika African National Union (TANU). The president called the idea a unique identity of African society, arguing that in contemporary Africa, just as in egalitarian societies, there were no real class conflicts; and therefore, a multiparty system had no reason to exist: "In African society, the traditional method of conducting affairs is by free discussion. Elders sit under the big tree and talk until they agree" (Nyerere, 1966, p. 105). The big tree in this case would imply the only ruling political party. If President Nyerere were still alive in the twenty-first century, he would have a rude awaking. The social dynamic of Tanzania has changed.

More changes occurred during the presidency of Julius Nyerere a few years later. On January 29, 1967, the Tanzanian government passed the Arusha Declaration Policies on Socialism and Self-Reliance. The declaration was Tanzania's most prominent political statement of African socialism. The declaration also involved the Leadership Code, to promote equality among all Tanzanian citizens. The code was one of several attempts to prevent party leaders and well-to-do individuals from forming privileged and exploitative groups. The overall goal of the Arusha Declaration policies was to reduce income inequality among all citizens and shift development efforts toward the rural areas. With the support of the TANU, the Arusha Declaration argued that the country was involved in a war against ignorance, poverty, and disease.

The Arusha Declaration also emphasized Ujamaa; which was the centerpiece of the Social and Economic Development program developed by Julius Kamarage Nyerere, first president of Tanzania. *Ujamaa* is a Swahili word that means "family-hood or brotherhood." In the Ujamaa program, groups of village families worked together on communal farms for the common good. While it is true that significant improvements occurred in Tanzania from the Arusha Declaration policies, there were more challenges for the country. By the mid-1980s the Tanzanian government realized that its development policies and strategies had proved to be a failure when it came to socioeconomic development. In 1986 the government, which was previously resistant, gave in and agreed to the IMF and World Bank reform package aimed at providing economic assistance. Although the policies of the IMF/World Bank package were at loggerheads with key components of the policy of socialism and self-reliance outlined in the 1967 Arusha Declaration, the Tanzanian government realized the need for reform.

Increasing political and economic development led to further sidelining of the Arusha Declaration policies. An example was the Zanzibar Resolution of 1991, which did away with an important pillar of the Arusha Declaration: The Leadership Code. Experts argued that the failure the Arusha Declaration policies was attributed to both external and internal factors. The conclusion from the point of view of opponents of the policies is that socialism had failed and capitalism was winning, and winning fast. That being the case, something had to be put in place to sustain the Tanzanian democracy. In 1995, the government appointed a group of experts to formulate a policy document in consultation with different sections of the Tanzanian community at large. The outcome of the effort was the creation of a new vision known as the Tanzania Development Vision 2025. The aims are to guide Tanzanian development efforts into the twenty-first century and achieve certain development levels by the year 2025 (Mallya, 2014).

According to the vision, Tanzania is expected to achieve the following by 2025:

- Have a population with a high quality of life
- Be a stable, peaceful, and united country
- Have intact, well-functioning good governance machinery
- Have a well-educated population that craves learning
- Have a competitive economy capable of producing sustainable growth and shared benefits

Critics argued that lots of issues needed to be sorted out before anything spectacular could happen in the next twenty-five years. One of those issues was what opponents of the vision called the failure of the Arusha Declaration policies that were in use for thirty years, from 1967 until 1997. The general assessment of the Arusha Declaration is that Tanzania was neither socialist nor self-reliant. Secondly, the three enemies that then-Tanganyika had declared war against in 1961, poverty, disease, and ignorance, are still rampant in the country. Some believe that poverty has increased, an issue that is common in other African counties. Critics also argue that there is nothing new about in Vision 2025 that was not covered in the Arusha Declaration policies of 1967. However, there are some differences in the two policies. The environment of the Vision 2025 is not the same compared to the Arusha Declaration of 1967. The other differentiator is the social dynamic of the country, meaning much different perspectives of the people compared to thirty years ago. Public policy can be experimental but to make it possible, leaders with commitment, integrity, and political courage are required. The questions that remain when it comes to Vision 2025 are: What is likely to be the stimulus and force behind the implementation of the vision? And secondly, will it need donors, or will the vision prescription be owned by the people?

USAID'S MISSION IN TANZANIA

In the United States International Development program, good governance is a priority. Although Tanzania is one of Africa's most politically stable and peaceful countries, its institutionalized democracy and good governance are challenged by issues of corruption and poor delivery of government services. However, with threshold funding from Millennium Challenge Corporation (MCC), United States Agency for International Development's (USAID) mission supports Tanzania's Democracy and Good Governance programs by providing the $698 million compact that was signed in 2008. The USAID's mission has built in these achievements by increasing the capacity of civil society to monitor accountability and transparency in local government by engaging citizens in budgeting, planning, and public expenditure tracking (Sengo, 2014). The mission also supports the Tanzanian government's ability to improve accountability and oversight of public resources through increased citizen participation. Involving citizens in issues that affect their lives is a major step in improving government services.

Another area supported by the USAID's mission is governance and the rule of law. Supporting the rule of law and human rights, the mission provides financial and technical training to improve justice through grass-roots legal aid clinics. The program focuses primarily on women and other vulnerable groups. The legal aid services are intended to improve justice for women who remain unprotected from violent partners. The program also supports widows of partners with HIV/AIDS who are left without an inheritance or denied custody of children; offenders who are incarcerated without access to legal defense, and HIV-positive individuals suffering from discrimination. The AIDS epidemic affects a number of African nations, but in some countries the disease is more prevalent. Between 2012 and 2013, USAID's mission in Tanzania trained 265 legal aid providers and human rights defenders who provided free legal services to 518 women and 226 men. During that same period, USAID missions also built local capacity through a partnership with the Tanzania Network of Legal Aid Providers, an indigenous umbrella organization. The current goal is to reach more than a million people with events in 340 villages.

USAID PARTNERSHIP WITH CIVIL SOCIETY IN TANZANIA

USAID in partnership with the Tanzanian government supports civil society institutions in the country by strengthening their oversight operations, increasing their interactions with citizens, and conducting outreach activities. The efforts also support civil society work and make their reports and sources of information more accessible to the public. The role of civil society is relevant in developing public policy. The initiative is meant to ensure sustainable democratic processes and provide greater domestic accountability among the institutions and people-centered policy making. The policy helps to create a healthy civil society in Tanzania. USAID has also developed the capacity and sustainability of Tanzanian civil society organizations to enhance citizen demand for transparency and accountability in the allocation and use of public resources. USAID and the Tanzanian government's joint effort is currently focused in the Morogoro, Dodoma, Iringa, Mtwara, and Zanzibar regions.

In examining the viability and sustainability of the democratic experiment in Tanzania, experts believed there are three major points to remember. The first is the nature of the state and the manner in which Tanzanians relate to it. This assessment is based on judging the forty-eight years of post-independence experimentation in state and nation building. One can say that a "Tanzanian identity" has emerged. That identity is growing in stature and importance in Africa and the global circle. The second point has to do with the role of civil society in the consolidation of the democratic spirit in Tanzanian lives and culture. It is fair to assert that many Tanzanians can implant the spirit in their daily lives and the activities of their organizations. Democracy cannot take place in any society if the people are not willing to plant the seeds in the areas of life frequented by the youth. The third point is that consolidation of democracy among Tanzanians will depend on the development of the political system.

REMEMBERING JULIUS NYERERE

Mwalimu Julius Kambarage Nyerere was born in Butiama near Lake Victoria on April 13, 1922. He was first president and father of Tanganyika independence on December 9, 1961, and for its unity with Zanzibar on April 26, 1964, to create the United Republic of Tanzania. The late Tanzanian leader was also the father of southern African liberation, one of the nine leaders who came together in 1980 to establish the Southern Africa Development Coordination Conference (SADCC), which later became the Southern African Development Community (SADC). When Nyerere died on October 14, 1999, at the age of seventy-seven, Africans everywhere shared the Tanzanians' sense of loss. Julius Nyerere was known as Baba Wataifa, meaning "father of the nation." Nyerere was a charismatic leader with a sharp intellect and great personal integrity. He welded a country and a national identity from over 120 ethnic groups, united by their Swahili language and a social harmony constructed on the ideas of peace, justice, unity, and personal commitment, according to the Southern African Research and Documentation Center (1985).

Julius Nyerere's support for equality and tolerance ranged across all races, religions, classes, and genders, as was evident by political independence through nonviolence. His legacies include encouragement for Tanzanian women to assume leadership roles in society and the adoption of a parliamentary system that guaranteed seats for women. He worked tirelessly in support of this goal that achieved political independence for Zambia and Malawi in 1964; Botswana and Lesotho in 1966; Mauritius and Swaziland in 1968, and Seychelles in 1976. When the other countries in southern Africa were struggling for liberation from colonial rule, Tanzania provided political, material, and moral support until independence and majority rule was achieved in Mozambique and Angola (1975), Zimbabwe (1980), Namibia (1990), and finally in South Africa (1994). His commitment to the liberation of Africa from white minority rule was demonstrated by allowing several liberation movements to establish their bases in Tanzania. For example, the African National Congress (ANC) had a base in Arusha, Tanzania. Other liberation movements that had bases in Tanzania include the Pan Africanist Congress (PAC), the Frente de Libertá led by Samora Machel of Mozambique, and the Zimbabwe African National Union (ZANU).

President Nyerere was committed to the ideas of liberation, democracy, and common humanity for the rest of the continent, along with leaders of other African countries that were already independent in 1963. They established the OAU, now the African Union. Under the chairmanship of Julius Nyerere, the leaders of Zambia, Tanzania, and Botswana formed the Front Line States to work together in a united front for common security and for majority rule in neighboring countries in 1974. The Front Line States served as the forerunner of the SADC organ on politics, defense, and security cooperation. Although the decision to initiate what became SADC was conceptualized in Arusha, Tanzania, it was later launched in Lusaka, Zambia. The organization was hosted by Botswana, and Nyerere selflessly used any occasion to give credit for its formation to his colleague and close friend, late president of Botswana Seretse Khama. Julius Nyerere retired as president Tanzania in 1985 and as chairman of the party (Chama Cha Mapinduzi) in 1990.

Up to the time of his death, Nyerere worked hard to strengthen developmental links between the developing countries of southern Africa. Between 1987 and 1990, he chaired the Southern Africa Commission and dedicated the next decade of his life to the service of south-central

Africa and tirelessly did fundraising for a capital fund and operation cost. Julius Nyerere often said that his generation had achieved at least one goal, political liberation of Africa, and that the next generation must take up the next goal. When he died, a long memorial was read by his close friend and colleague Dr. Kenneth Kaunda, the former president of Zambia, reminding all of Africa that the best way to mourn his death was to carry on where he left off (Southern African Research and Development Center, 1985).

SOUTH AFRICA: A LOOK AT DEMOCRACY AND ECONOMIC GROWTH

When it comes to peaceful transitions to a democratic process, there are few countries that can be compared to South Africa. Collectively, the people of South Africa have secured a firm place in history in the twenty-first century for realizing their vision of a just and inclusive democracy through reconciliation rather than retribution, given its brutal history of liberation struggle. An interview conducted in 2001 with a diverse group of black leaders in the new dispensation shows that transition was the result of the collective choice of individuals and groups. The youth also played a key role in this process.

The 2001 interview was part of an ongoing program aimed at exploring pathways by which individuals can become leaders in their community, organization, government, or religious institution. People interviewed came from government and nongovernment organizations; they also came from rural and urban areas, employed and unemployed. They shared their experiences that led to the current level of civil activism. For many blacks in South Africa, the experiences endured under white hegemony and under colonial and apartheid rule, when they were relegated and humiliated as second-class citizens in their own homeland. To move forward in the new dispensation, it was necessary to create such a program. Consequently, it paved the way for true reconciliation among the people.

After over three hundred years of white domination of the country's majority black population, South Africa made a remarkable change to democratic governance by holding multiparty and multiethnic elections in 1994, resulting in the election of Nelson Mandela as its first indigenous president. Since that historic event, South Africa has negotiated two democratic constitutions and held five successful national elections. Despite such political progress in recent years, the government of South Africa faces a number of challenges, both economically and socially. However, the government continues to improve the situation to stabilize the increasing debt and reverse the double digit-inflation that was inherited from the apartheid regime. Since the 1990s, the South African economy has shed over 500,000 jobs, with an economic growth of 3 percent and an overall unemployment estimated at 30 percent (Guseh and Oritsejafor, 2005). Another challenge is the lack of business confidence that is slowing down domestic and foreign investment, plus an increase in inequality within each of the racial groups.[2]

THE IMPACT OF MANDELA'S LIFETIME ON AFRICA:

An argument can be made that in the ninety-five years of Nelson Mandela's life encompass the transition from colonialism to independence on the continent. Mandiba was born on a continent that was colonized and in servitude to European powers, with the exception of Ethiopia and Liberia, the only independent nations, till the middle of the twentieth century, when most of Africa was free from colonial rule. The defeat of Germany in World War II brought about a major transition, resulting in the reworking of the colonial order when its possessions, what became present-day Tanzania, Cameroon, Tago, Burundi, and Rwanda, were distributed among the war's victorious powers. Those powers included Great Britain, France, and Belgium (McGreal, 2013). Subsequently, German Southwest Africa, which is present day Namibia, eventually fell under the control of South Africa (also known as Azania). Nelson Mandela was now a citizen of a new country; a country he would spend nearly half of his life transforming.

---

[2] **Gordon, Diana R**. *Contemporary Justice Review,* "Deepening Democracy Through Community Dispute Resolution: Problems And Prospects in South Africa and Chile," Sept. 2011, Vol. 14, Issue 3, p. 291–305..

Between 1936 and 1945 a major development happened in Ethiopia, when Italian fascist dictator Benito Mussolini invaded one of Africa's oldest countries. The invasion of Ethiopia without provocation confirmed that the League of Nations was a toothless world body in the face of aggression by one of its members. Consequently, Ethiopia was integrated into Italian East Africa with Eritrea and Italian Somaliland. A few years after the Italian invasion in 1940, a three-year desert war raged across North Africa, swinging from French Tunisia and Italian Libya within striking distance of Cairo, Egypt. With the impact of World War II, Africa was experiencing colonialism at the highest degree. The conflict had already made the colonial map, forcing Italy to relinquish its rule of Libya and Somalia. In 1941, Ethiopia was liberated from Italy. After World War II, France recovered its possession of Tunisia where a majority of the expatriate population resided. The French authority was fatally undermined, and Tunisia obtained its independence, along with Morocco, within a few years (McGreal, 2013, p.18).

During World War II, many African soldiers served the allied cause in North and East Africa, Europe, and Asia. These soldiers returned home from the war questioning the discontent between the very allies whose interests were served with the continued subjugation of their own continent. I am sure Mandela and others who became young men during this period realized the impact colonialism was having on the continent. The anticolonial leaders had an important argument to make in their struggles. These leaders found a direction to draw strength from and became increasingly empowered to struggle for their freedom. What became South Africa had been born eight years earlier with the unification of four existing British colonies already. That unification also included two former Afrikaner republics, the Transvaal and the Orange Free State that were taken over after the Boer War. Interestingly, the Boer War was the beginning of the anticolonial struggle that eventually became the fight of Mandela and the ANC.

One of Mandela's biggest anticolonial struggles was due to the large white population in South Africa, with an autonomous political dominion under the British crown, unlike Great Britain's other African colonies with fewer whites. Liberia before independence was considered by the British as a commercial interest and a philanthropic organization; some territories in southern Africa were regarded as the private property of commercial companies in 1918 (McGreal, 2013). For example, Southern Rhodesia, which is now present-day Zimbabwe, was owned by the British South Africa Company; therefore, it was not recognized as a British colony until 1923. The history of the apartheid system, or separation of the races, began in 1948. It happened when the National Party won power in South Africa with an unexpected and narrow victory. On the party's platform was a more rigid race segregation agenda. The leaders of the National Party, predominantly Afrikaners still bitter about the Boer War and the loss of self-determination, created the apartheid system as the way to enforce racial separation. The Afrikaners portrayed the apartheid system as a form of social well-being for poorer whites.

The system was also intended to protect white workers from cheaper black labor. The issue of job protection for one group of people against others would have been a nonissue if the government were inclusive and served all of its citizens. Also on record against the Afrikaner leaders was the British prime minister, Harold Macmillan, in his speech to the South African Parliament in 1960 in Cape Town. The prime minister said that apartheid government was on the wrong side of history. South Africa left the British Commonwealth the following year because of Britain's position.

South Africa was a nation blessed with tremendous natural resources, such as gold, rubber, tobacco, diamonds, ivory, and copper. Part of Mandela and the ANC's argument, among other issues, include a decision-making process that ensured the fair use of country's wealth for all South Africans. The efforts of the ANC and Mandel, plus thousands of South Africans, helped to raise political awareness and challenge white claims of racial superiority. In his entire lifetime, Nelson Mandela maintained a position against racial domination, be it white or black. He believed that South Africa belonged to all South Africans, a philosophy he stood and fought for till his death.

Africa as a continent became primed to experience major moves toward rapid decolonization. The decolonization period in most of Africa helped to drive the white regime's increasingly repressive response to resistance to apartheid policy. Consequently, the resistance led to the arrest and trial of Mandela and other ANC leaders like Oliva Tambo, Walter Sisulu, etc.

The 1950s was a period when decolonization engulfed sub-Sahara Africa, beginning on the Gold Coast with the rebirth of Ghana in 1957. More progressive was Ghana's first Prime Minister, Dr. Kwame Nkrumah, who promoted the idea of Pan Africa, inspiring other nations that were still under colonial rule. The movement for independence spread to other parts of Africa, especially in countries where there were large numbers of white settlements. What was most intriguing during the decolonization period was determination of some African countries to negotiate or fight for their independence, for example the Mau Mau rebellion in Kenya to end British rule in East Africa. Within a few years, most former British colonies in Africa became countries that had gained independence or were on the brink of obtaining it.

By 1956 another colonial power had given up control of two of its colonies in North Africa. The Arab colonies of Tunisia and Morocco became independent, followed by Algeria. In North Africa, Algeria, a country that Paris regarded as a department of France, was home to close to one million white settlers (McGreal, 2013). The Algerian situation became a civil war and brought down France's fourth republic and stripped Paris of its colonial belief. The Algerian civil war helped to remove any lingering hopes of France holding onto its sub-Saharan colonies. The burst of independence freed most of French Africa in 1960. Belgium, seeing the coming rude awakening, pulled out of the Democratic Republic of the Congo in that same year, followed by Rwanda and Burundi a couple of years later. Interestingly, France made sure to hold its former colonies close to her by maintaining economic, political, and military ties, including the introduction of regional currencies. The movement for independence that swept across the continent did not go down without a fight. As the imperial powers withdrew, some of the settler administrations were determined to carry on. For example, in Rhodesia (now Zimbabwe), the white minority government of Ian Smith decided to unilaterally declare its independence on November 11, 1965, in resistance to the United Kingdom's plan to keep the colony dependent.

The United Kingdom declared the move by Rhodesia an act of treason. Backing Rhodesia was Portugal and apartheid South Africa, giving Rhodesia economic assistance and allowing Portugal access through its ports in Mozambique. Despite the assistance from South Africa and

Portugal, in the 1970s Rhodesia was still besieged by sanctions, coupled with an escalation of insurgency. The policy was eventually changed when Mozambique became independent and provided a base for Robert Mugabe's ZANU guerrillas. Robert Mugabe became Zimbabwe's first president; a position he has held since 1980. The independent movement that launched rebellions in the 1960s helped to set free the last three Portuguese territories: Angola, Mozambique, and Guinea-Bissau. In the following decade much disappointment was seen across Africa in the Cold War struggle. The Soviet Union backed African liberation movements. The Soviet backing was countered in a number of African countries by American support for military coups and authoritarian leadership. During the Cold War era, Western aid based on anti-communist credentials with little concern about good governance and democratic reform was the order of the day.

A period when Western aid was given to military dictatorships and one-party states run by leaders for life surfaced from Liberia to Malawi, from Kenya to Ivory Coast (Côte d'Ivoire), from Zaire to Zambia. At the same time the Soviets were supporting governments including Mozambique and Ethiopia (McGreal, 2014). The bloodiest Cold War confrontation in Africa occurred in Angola, with Soviet-backed government and Cuban troops fighting a long war against Jonas Savimbi's rebels and South African–army troops sponsored by the United States government. The conflict killed thousands of Africans and destroyed towns and villages in this oil-rich nation, causing thousands of people to flee their homes. This was a period when some of the world most brutal and extreme leaders evolved, such as General Idi Amin, the military dictator of Uganda (regarded as part clown and part monster), and Mobutu Sese Seko of Zaire. Mobutu was accused of stealing billions of dollars while the country collapsed (McGreal, 2014; p. 6).

Nelson Mandela's release from prison in 1990 caused a wave of expectation among many people across the continent who were weary of mismanagement and seeking good governance. Another issue the continent was facing was political leaders who were determined to hold on to power. The expectation of a new and better day forced old leaders from power across Africa in countries such as Kenya, Zambia, Malawi, Zaire, Liberia, and Uganda, among others. The new wave of expectation was not successful everywhere. For example, in Nigeria, it resulted in a number of military coups. Another setback was the dependence on foreign aid from Western nations with strings attached. Some African countries were already suffering from the imposition of International Monetary Fund and the World Bank economic plans. The conditions of these plans were harsh on the poorest people, especially when the benefits they enjoyed were reversed, including free schooling, health care, and other assistance that people were receiving.

Many African countries were forced to privatize their programs and other measures to meet the demands of the economic plans. These measures caused enormous hardship, which undermined needed support provided by most of the newly elected democratic governments. Therefore, foreign aid was no longer considered a savior but rather an obstacle to international development.

Mandela was elected as the first black president of South Africa in 1994 and set an example by stepping down after five years in office, something most African leaders (past and present) have not been able to do. He was succeeded by his deputy, Thabo Mbeki, who was regarded by most in the West as a steady pair of hands with a strong intellect. On the other hand, Mbeki received criticism for his outlandishly remote views of the AIDS epidemic and for siding with Zimbabwe's lifelong president, Robert Mugabe.

BURKINA FASO: WEST AFRICAN SPRING

Overview

Burkina Faso, which is also commonly known as Burkina, is a landlocked country in West Africa. It is about 274,200 square kilometers, equivalent to 105,900 square miles. Burkina Faso is surrounded by six countries: Mali to the north; Niger to the east; Benin to the southeast; Togo and Ghana to the south; and Ivory Coast to the southwest. The seat of government is Ouagadougou, located at the center of the country. As of 2013, its population was estimated at 16,934, 839. The country was formerly called the Republic of Upper Volta and later renamed Burkina Faso in 1984 by then-president Thomas Sankara. *Burkina Faso* combines words from each of the two major languages: Moore and Dioula. In the Moore language, *Burkina* means "men of integrity" and *Faso*, from the Dioula language, translates as "fatherland." Burkina Faso is understood as "land of upright people" or "land of honest people." The residents of Burkina Faso are Burkinbe people. The official language of government and business is French.

According to African ancient history, between 14000 and 5000 BC, Burkina Faso was populated by hunter-gatherers in the country's northwestern region. Settlements of farmers appeared between 2600 and 3600 BC. What is now central Burkina Faso was primarily composed of Mossi kingdoms. In 1896 France established a protectorate over the kingdoms in this territory. After independence in 1960, the country's governmental structures underwent many changes, but today it is a semi-presidential republic. The former president is Blaise Compaoré, who has been in this position since 1987 after a coup by an armed gang killed Thomas Sankara and twelve other officials. It was alleged that the coup was organized by Sankara's former colleague and childhood friend, the former president of the country, but he continues to deny it, arguing that Sankara's death was unintentional. According to the president, the decision to kill Sankara was due to the deterioration of relations with neighboring countries. Blaise Compaoré also argued that Sankara jeopardized relations with France, the former colonial power, and neighboring Ivory Coast, another former French colony. The United States, France, and Liberia were widely suspected of helping to orchestrate the coup that killed Sankara (Badger, 2014). A former Liberian warlord, Prince Johnson, told the Liberian Truth and Reconciliation Commission (TRC) allies that the coup was engineered by Charles Taylor, a former warlord and president of Liberia.

Since independence in 1960, Burkina Faso has gone through a series of bloody coups, including a Marxist-inspired revolution in 1983 that installed the communist leader Thomas Sankara as president. Sankara was very popular among the working class of the country, especially for his support for women's rights. During his leadership, he instituted a number of radical social reforms, ranging from efforts to abolish gender inequality in the country and promoting a policy of self-reliance among the people.

While the reform efforts received support among the poorer sectors of the society, they also created enemies among the economic elites. Sankara also faced numerous challenges on the international stage during his leadership because of his policies. In December 1985, a territorial dispute brought a war, known as the Christmas War, between Mali and Burkina. The dispute was over a 100-mile-long portion of desert, rich with minerals, referred to as Agacher Strip. In addition, Sankara pitted Burkina Faso against the interests of Western superpowers and their African allies, which was a recipe for disaster for the young revolutionary leader.

Sankara was an outspoken opponent of South Africa's apartheid system and military raids against the ANC in Botswana, Zambia, and Zimbabwe. Outside of Africa, the Burkinabe leader also expressed solidarity with the Palestine Liberation Organization (PLO) and Nicaragua's Sandinistas. Burkina Faso's ties with Libya and Ghana prompted the United States and France to fear that the "Burkinabe model" would spread throughout the continent of Africa. Between 1983 and 1990, Paris canceled foreign assistance to Ouagadougou, the capital. Under their leader, Burkina Faso turned to its former colonial master, France, for international support, as opposed to Russia and Cuba. These changes allowed Burkina Faso to export its natural resources and created a stable political climate for investment. However, the country was totally isolated. Burkina Faso is a member of a number of international and regional organizations, including the AU, the Community of Sahel-Saharan States, La Francophonie, the Organization of Islamic Cooperation, and the Economic Community of West African States (ECOWAS).

Burkina Faso, like most African nations, faces challenges, including combating corruption, strengthening political parties, improving electoral processes, and good governance. After more than two decades as leader of Burkina Faso, President Blaise Compaoré is not allowed to run for the presidency in 2015, according to the current constitution. Another challenge Burkina Faso faces is the social explosion. Its society is one the fastest growing societies in Africa, with increasing modernization and globalization creating high expectations in the young population for change. Despite strong economic growth, there is a need to address the issues of the widespread inequalities that are making Burkina Faso one of the poorest counties in the world. In the midst of all the challenges, Burkina

Faso still enjoys a certain level of popularity in the sub-Sahara region. It holds a significant diplomatic influence in West Africa. According to *Africa Report* (2013), under its current leadership Burkina Faso has become a key player in resolution of regional crises. The president and his team have succeeded with much ingenuity in positioning themselves as indispensable mediators in West Africa. It also served as a watchdog in helping Western countries monitor the security situation in the Sahel and the Sahara.

Instability in Burkina Faso would not only lead to loss of a key ally and a strategic base for France and the United States, it would also reduce the capacity of the African country for dealing with regional conflicts. Experts report the collapse of the Burkinabe diplomatic apparatus would also mean the loss of an important reference point in West Africa, which despite other challenges and limitations has played a critical role as a regulatory authority in the region. The Burkinabe government has responded to the challenges by implementing reforms that have not met popular expectations. In 1998, the government initiated a series of political reforms, including an independent electoral commission, a single-ballot voting system, public campaign financing, and a third vice-presidential position in the legislature for opposition leaders. In 2000, a two-term presidential limit was reinstituted by the government, but the law was not retroactive, allowing the former president to be re-elected for a third term in 2005. The international partners of Burkina Faso, especially Western allies, should no longer focus exclusively on the current leader's mediation role and monitoring security risks in West Africa; they should also give attention to domestic politics and the promotion of democratic processes in the country.

The role of civil society in the reform effort is critical. It has a network of young people who are dedicated to building a more just, accountable, and prosperous Burkina Faso. Yam Pukri is a civil society and technology association that provides its portal services online for democracy and good governance in the country. Burkina Faso also houses a capacity-building institution, a training center for local officials from fifteen West African nations. The primary goals of the center are to develop the skills of local councilors through education and exchange, help improve local governments, set up networks of towns, and monitor and assess the impact of its training sessions (*University World News*, 2010). Another initiative is the Burkina Faso Urban Country Program undertaken by the Burkinabe government. The objective is to align urban development efforts at the national government, local government, and community levels, including the urban poor in the planning and decision-making process (Cities Alliance n.d.). Because of the high rate of illiteracy, especially among rural officials—nearly 16,000 individuals according to UNDP—the agency, in partnership with the government, piloted literacy campaigns in forty communities.

The initiative, which was partly funded by UNDP, was led by the Ministry for Basic Education and Literacy Training and the Ministry of Regional Government and Decentralization (UNDP, 2009). The report asserts that additional challenges are affecting the reform efforts, such as weak technical capacity and poor support mechanisms for decentralized services and territorial communities, challenges that are common across the continent. In an attempt to mitigate the challenges, UNDP pointed to the need to mobilize resources to finance the decentralization process. It is believed that the measures will improve literacy skills and widen the distribution of informative text that will guide the decentralization process. In 2010 a report by the World Bank concluded that local governments have a very low degree of discretionary power and weak accountability to citizens at all levels. The lack of discretionary power is also due to strongly centralized power in most unitary governments in Africa. In the fiscal sphere, Burkina Faso's taxing powers are restricted, making local financial management extremely difficult (*Journal of Public Administration and Development*, 2010).

In 2013, the World Bank produced another report identifying eight major institutional challenges at the following levels:

- An unclear link between decentralization and de-concentration. Government agencies at the regional level are both national government and local government entities. The functions of the decentralized regions do not seem clear despite a list of devolved responsibilities.
- A lack of democratic legitimacy within the regional assemblies, as these representatives are indirectly elected by their peers, thereby risking a lack of autonomy from the local governments. Such a risk

is increased by the communes, which collect the taxes and then transfer only a small share or percent of the receipts to the regions.

Feeding a central government at the expense of local governments is common in Africa. However, the Burkinabe government is working hard to reform its political process to address these issues (World Bank, 2013). Burkina Faso's strong economic growth is sometimes overshadowed by concern over widespread inequalities in the country. These situations have created public distrust, sparking violent protests in 2011 involving various segments of the society, including rank-and-file soldiers in several cities across the country.

The death of student Justin Zongo while in police custody in February 2011 brought about student riots in many major cities. In reaction to the incident, the government ordered universities to close down and cut off funding for student services. Meanwhile, army soldiers mutinied over three months of unpaid wages and also caused a period of looting and violence nationwide. In April of the same year, policemen and teachers joined the protests, demanding better pay and working conditions. Resistance in organizations can sometimes bring about positive change and improvement. A number of reform efforts in Burkina Faso may be contributed to resistance from the citizens. In most African governments, sometimes the response from the public is undemocratic.

ETHIOPIA: FROM DICTATORSHIP TO DEMOCRACY

As one of Africa's oldest independent nations, Ethiopia has seen its share of fallen dictators. But Ethiopia is not alone on the continent when it comes to a transition from decades of dictatorial government to democratic reform. In just a few years we have seen the fall of dictators, from Ben Ali of Tunisia being rooted out after twenty-four years of rule; Hosni Mubarak thrown out and hauled into court after thirty-two years, and Moamar Gadhafi of Libya literally dragged out of the sewers and paraded in the streets of Tripoli and executed with his own golden pistol.

In sub-Sahara Africa, we also saw Laurent Gbagbo of Ivory Coast held up in his palace and Charles Taylor of Liberia turned over to the International

Criminal Court to face charges against humanity. The list of fallen dictators in sub-Sahara Africa includes Moadou Tandja of Niger, who tried to cling to power by ignoring constitutional term limits, and recently, eighty-five-year-old Abdoulaye Wade of Senegal, after attempting to steal a third term in office facing a firestorm of public protest (Marian, 2012). As Al Marian asked in a weekly column in 2011, "What happens to African fallen dictators after the mud walls of dictatorship come tumbling down and the palaces of illusion behind those walls vanish?" He answered that they would pick their bags and fly off like bats and hide out in the backyards of their brother dictators who are still in power or remain fugitives from justice. What will happen to Ethiopia since its mud walls of dictatorship have fallen? Will she face Libya's fate, Egypt's, or Tunisia's? There is a decisive role to be played by all sectors of Ethiopian society and friends of Ethiopia in sharing a post-dictatorship Ethiopia. They include individual Ethiopian groups, civil society, independent press institutions, prodemocracy activists, human rights advocates, political parties, and grassroots organizations. All these groups must come together to spearhead dialogue and debate on Ethiopia's transition from a one-man, one-party dictatorship to a genuine multiparty democracy that is grounded in the rule of law. In response to the reform efforts in Ethiopia, a group of grassroots civil organizations known as the Ethiopian National Transition Council (ENTC) has stepped up and accepted the challenge of thinking through a possible democratic reform after the collapse of the mud walls of dictatorship in Africa's oldest independent nation.

The ENTC seeks to mobilize and engage Ethiopians from all walks of life in a dialogue and debate over how to transition to a democratic political process. The grassroots organization aims to "facilitate the process of collaboration, consensus building, networking, and information dissemination" to a mixed group of stakeholders in the society (Marian, 2012). As a civil organization, the Ethiopian National Transition Council is not connected to any political party, nor does it have any political ambitions besides advocating for democratic governance and respect for basic human rights in the country. The role of civil society is bringing about reform and good governance across the continent, and Ethiopian is no exception. The primary goal of the ENTC is to become an independent and inclusive civil society with the agenda of helping to establish a free, democratic, peaceful, and prosperous Ethiopia. One of the individuals at the forefront of ENTC is an extraordinary young man, Dr. Fiseha Eshetu, with tremendous achievements in the Ethiopian higher education system, resulting in the largest privately owned, and fully accredited university.

GOVERNMENT REFORM EFFORTS IN ETHIOPIA

According to African Development Bank (ADB), the government of Ethiopia has embarked on a number of comprehensive civil service reform programs designed to improve performance and strengthen accountability, and transparency. In order to ensure broad-based reform efforts to improve effectiveness in public service delivery and advance the democratization process, the Ethiopian government has initiated a decentralization program. The laws, rules, and regulations of the civil service have undergone changes in line with the 1995 federal constitution to foster an impartial, ethical, accountable civil service (ADB, 2009). Another area of a high degree of compliance measures is the payroll system, which is relatively strong. Since the country's new constitution was adopted in 1994, Ethiopia has held three national elections. The government has undertaken measures since the last elections to further enhance the democratic process. The third multiparty elections took place in May 2005. The elections of 2005 were judged by many as the most openly contested in the country's political history.

Although the ruling party won the elections, it had a significantly reduced majority in the parliament due to an unprecedented interest and turnout compared to the previous elections. As reform efforts become mature, Ethiopia will serve as another success story on the Horn of Africa. For several years, Ethiopia has enjoyed impressive economic growth. Education and health services are being expanded. There are many curves that point in the right direction due to the reform efforts. Massive housing construction projects are transforming cities and replacing corrugated-tin slums with flats. The capital, Addis Ababa, is one of the fastest-growing cities in the world. Market reforms and the introduction of new technologies have given rural famers the tools to raise themselves out of poverty. In the past, a farmer had to sell his or her crops to government agents, but now the producer can sell to anyone. With the new technologies, farmers can use cell phones to check the prices of products in their local areas. There is also a safety net in the form of food assistance from the Ethiopian government through partnership with donor agencies to assist citizens if there is lack of food before harvest or during a time of drought.

The government has produced a three-pronged plan to accelerate its development: (A) New hydropower projects to provide electricity for the rural areas and export earnings when excess electricity is sold abroad; (B) Expand the manufacturing industry to produce goods hitherto imported as finished goods, and (C) Produce sugar, rice, soybeans, and other crops in large plantations to turn Ethiopia's large imports into even greater exports to a richer and fatter world.

The effort by the government to use the sparsely populated lowland areas to increase growth and exports is critical and understandable as a means to create jobs for a growing population. However, there are still challenges that the country must address. Inflation in the country is sky-high. In the cities there is widespread discontent with unemployment and price hikes for basic commodities (Backlander, 2013). There is a lack of opportunities, especially for young people, an issue that is very common in most African countries with increasing urban immobility.

On the local level, the Ethiopian government has decentralized its governance structure known as the Woreda Council, which is the main representative body at the local level. The decisions of the council directly affect the welfare of citizens and local communities. Because of the dual accountability the council is subjected to, some have suggested relegating (or sending) community accountability to a secondary level, resulting in undermining the needs and interests of the community. Experts argued that dual accountability also limits the independence of the local council; as a result, the autonomy of the Woreda Council is not fully respected. A governance study carried out in 2003 showed that 44 percent of experts interviewed believed that mechanisms for local accountability were rarely effective and efficient.

The role of civil society in Ethiopia, as in most parts of Africa, is mainly engaged in humanitarian activities; however, in the past decades, the focus has shifted toward advocacy activities. The shift has created tension in relationships between the government and the civil society. The lack of transparency in funding and activities has been the cause of the uneasy relationship between the two entities. Civil society has primarily relied on donor financing, most often foreign donors with specific agendas focused on reforms. Some of the challenges civil society organizations face in Ethiopia includes the lack of capacity and resources needed to effectively influence public policy. This is not only a challenge in Ethiopian but for civil society organizations across the continent. Yet some of these civil organizations have proved extremely effective in the areas of HIV advocacy, social justice, and gender rights. The Ethiopian government is committed to promote civil society participation in the development process through capacity building and other interventions as part of its reform efforts. In 2008, the government drafted a new civil society law to properly regulate its activities. The government has reaffirmed that the civil society law has incorporated relevant international experience and served the interests of the country. Ethiopia has made remarkable progress when it comes to decentralization. The developmental role of the state has also been significant.

According to the governance report of 2009, there is reason for continued engagement in funding by the African Development Bank. The quality of public financial management has improved, and the amount of fiscal resources transferred to subnational government has also increased significantly. However, there are still challenges that are critical in securing major gains in the reform efforts. Inflation in the country is sky-high. In the cities there is widespread of discontent with unemployment and price hikes for basic commodities. Opportunities, especially for young people, are lacking (Backlander, 2013), an issue that is very common in most African countries that are facing increasing urban immobility. Other challenges include promoting full participation of civil society, improving access to information to enhance transparency, strengthening the capacity and independence of the judiciary, and addressing accountability issues of other key institutions.

GOOD GOVERNANCE: THE KEY TO STRENGTHENING INTEGRITY AND ACCOUNTABILITY IN KENYA

Overview

The area that is known as present-day Kenya was first occupied by Cushitic-speaking people from northern Africa around 2000 BC. According to historical accounts, the Kenyan coast was frequented by Arab traders interested in East Africa due to its proximity to the Arabian Peninsula who established Arab and Persian colonies by the first century AD. The Nilotic and Bantu tribes also moved into this region of East Africa during the first millennium AD. But the Nilotic and Bantu peoples settled in the rural part of the Kenya. Between the Bantu and Arabic language was the evolution of the Swahili language, which was developed as a lingua franca for trade between the different groups in this area. By 1498, when the Portuguese arrived, the Arabs had already dominated the coastal area, using the present-day Port of Mombasa as an important resupply stop for ships that were bound for the Far East. Due to the dominance of Islamic control under the Imam of Oman in the 1600s, the Portuguese gave way. However, another European influence in the area followed in the nineteenth century: The United Kingdom. According to Hornsby (2013), the colonial history of Kenya goes back to the Berlin Conference in 1885, when most of Africa was divided into territories among the European powers.

One of those powers was the British government, which founded the East African Protectorate in 1895, primarily for the purpose of opening the fertile highland to white settlers coming from Europe. During the colonial system, the white settlers were the voice of the government; Africans and Asians were banned from direct political participation until 1944. The British brought thousands of Indians to Kenya and Uganda to build the railway. After the railway was completed, these Indians subsequently settled in Kenya and Uganda, inviting their kith and kin, mainly traders from India, to join them. With such a complex dynamic of people, it was a clear recipe for disaster, given the level of inequality, especially for the majority Africans.

In an attempt to resist colonialism, in 1942 members of the Kikuyu, Embu, Meru and Kamba tribes took an oath of unity and secrecy to fight for freedom from British colonial rule. The Mau Mau Movement was founded and began with that oath. The Africans in Kenya started their long, hard road to gain national sovereignty. After a decade in the movement, Jomo Kanyatta, its leader, was imprisoned for seven years. In 1956, another leader of the movement, Dedan Kimathi, was arrested and subsequently hanged for his role in the Mau Mau uprising. By 1952, the resistance was unstoppable as thousands of Kenyans were incarcerated. In 1957, the first direct elections of Africans to the legislative council took place. In 1962, Jomo Kenyatta was released to become the first prime minister of Kenya. On December 12, 1963, Kenya became a republic, and Jomo Kenyatta was the country's first president. During the same year, Kenya became a member of the British Commonwealth.

CHALLENGES AFTER KENYA'S INDEPENDENCE

After its independence from Great Britain in 1963, for nearly five decades Kenya experienced gains in social and economic development as a functioning nation-state, holding regular elections. It has also survived by keeping its borders and political system intact and by avoiding open war with neighboring countries and internal military rule. While it is true that Kenya is a favorite site for Western aid, trade, investment, and tourism and has remained a closed security partner for Western governments, the government has been unable to achieve adequate living conditions for most of its citizens. Among its challenges are corruption, violence, and tribalism that politics have been unable to solve. Most of the key conflicts have been over land, money, power, economic policy, national autonomy, and the distribution of resources between classes and communities (Hornsby, 2013). However, between the early 1980s and early 2000s, the country's economic performance deteriorated significantly. The economic downturn negatively affected growth and worsened poverty. The per capita income, according to the Kenya Economic Survey and UNDP in 2003 was estimated to be below US$400, which was lower than the sub-Saharan Africa (SSA) average. Poverty levels rose from 49 percent to 56 percent over the same period of time.

The Kenyan Demographic and Health Survey conducted in 2003 indicated that infant mortality per 1,000 live births increased from 63 in 1990 to 78 in 2002. The survey also showed a decline in life expectancy from 57 years in 1986 to 47 years in 2000, due primarily to the near collapse of public health service delivery in addition to reduced family income and the HIV/AIDS epidemic. During this period, other human development and social indicators also declined in the country. As a result of this uphill battle, Kenya ranked 154 of 177 countries in the UNDP Human Development Index in 2002 (Kenya Economic Survey and UNDP, 2003). The non-income dimensions of poverty in the country also worsened. Like in most African countries, illiteracy rates dramatically increased as primary school enrollment rates declined in the 1990s. The economic deterioration created major decreases in the nutritional status of children under the age of three, increasing the percentage of stunted children in that age group from 29 percent in 1993 to 31 percent 2003. The percentage of children between the ages of twelve and twenty-three months who were fully vaccinated dropped from 79 percent in 1993 to 52 percent in 2003. Despite the challenges, the Kenyan economy has shown signs of a strong recovery as evidenced by the achievement of a DGP growth rate of 5.8 percent in the 2005/2006 fiscal year, up from 4.9 percent in the 2004/2005 fiscal year.

According to the Kenyan Economic Survey, the overall household poverty level remains considerably high. Kenya's wealth distribution, like most countries across the continent, is still disproportionate. In Kenya, the richest segment of the population comprises 10 percent of the households, which control more than 42 percent of national wealth, while the poorest 10 percent controls less than 1 percent, according to the survey. Part of the challenge includes allegations of high-level corruption in the country, creating strange relations with donor organizations such as the World Bank and other development partners. While the Kenyan government is taking the issue more seriously than it has in the past, donor agencies are still unconvinced that much progress has been made. Development partners are demanding clear proof that the government is committed to serious efforts by fighting graft, and if this is not forthcoming, funding will be withdrawn progressively. A decision to withdraw funding is detrimental to economic performance and the government's war against poverty.

CHALLENGES TO GOOD GOVERNANCE IN KENYA

One of the national challenges Kenya faces is its poverty-reduction measures. The government planned to eradicate poverty through the economy. But the economic growth program has endured short-term hardship. Despite this, the government is hopeful that the hardships will subside as the country develops and the economy improves (Kenya, 1999). Experts believe that economic growth per se may not be sufficient to reduce poverty. The issue of poverty has a multidimensional component, such as shortages of income and deprivation that must be dealt with to improve the standard and quality of life. According to Ongaro (2006), poor people tend to be clustered in the following categories:

- The landless
- The handicapped
- Households headed by people without formal education
- Pastoralists in drought-prone arid and semi-arid land (ASAL) districts
- Unskilled and semi-casual laborers
- AIDS orphans
- Street children and the homeless

In the forty-three years since independence, the government of Kenya has put plans and measures in place to address the national challenge of poverty and other social development issues; however, poverty remains a key problem. Much credit must be given to Kenya for its efforts to bring about reform. Although Kenya remains among the committed nations in Africa, it is in the process of implementing its development blueprint known as Vision 2030, following the footstep of Tanzania. Vision 2030 is anchored by economic, social, and political pillars. Some of the keys aspects of the vision are reforms in governance and the public sectors. Included in the good governance policy is the plan for the government to intensify efforts to bring about attitudinal changes in public service that value transparency and accountability to the citizens of Kenya. Other measures being addressed in the Vision plan are corruption, gender equality, strengthening the local media, strengthening the civil society, tracking HIV/AIDS and other diseases, and building strong partnerships with development partners. Evidently, efforts are being made the government of

Kenya and its development partners to create an institutional infrastructure for good governance, which is the aim of the proposed project.

The aim of the institutional project is to support judiciary reforms in Kenya to include the procurement and auditing systems. The Kenyan government has also taken many bold steps to promote good governance. Those steps include the passing of several legislations, setting up appropriate institutions, and giving these institutions the legal authority to deal with anti-good-governance tendencies. There are several development partners harmonizing their support in the area of promoting good governance in Kenya (Ongaro, 2006). Although good governance and total reform have not yet been achieved in Kenya, an argument can be made that the country is heading in the right direction. Much progress has been made, but much remains to be done before such a goal can be realized.

Not too long ago Kenyans were still disputing election results, most recently the disputed 2007 general election, which degenerated into an unprecedented seven-week-long period of violence in parts of the country, including the Nairobi, the capital. The violence led to the loss of lives, dislocation of some citizens, destruction of property, and disruption of social and economic life. Reconciliation during the unrest brought top diplomats, such as former United Nations Secretary General Kofi Annan, president of Tanzania and chairman of the African Union Jakaya Kikwee, and other leaders from the region. It will take some time to establish trust in Kenyan society given its ugly past. On the other hand, if Kenyans are to attain sustainable economic and social development, according to experts, all Kenyans must work together toward making the idea of democratic reform a reality.[3]

---

[3] Wilfred A. Ongaro (Ph.D.) Editor December 2006,Good Governance and poverty Reduction Measures: A case study of Kenya, 2006.
3. Human Rights Watch Organization:
[Please include the footnote number in the correct position and format as appropriate.] Human Rights Watch is an international nongovernmental organization that conducts research and advocacy on human rights.

DEMOCRACY IN SENEGAL

Since attaining independence from France in 1960, Senegal has maintained a liberal democratic constitutional system of government. It has promoted a multiparty system as the political process norm. Senegal has a legacy from its colonial history of a group of intelligent and well-educated people who guide the political, artistic, and social processes. It is a country of ethnic and religious diversity that is free from national bias on issues. As a result, it has a tradition of pluralism and a highly organized civil society, such as unions, students, academics, and other professionals. The pluralistic character of the country is expressed through lively and elitist means. This openness is demonstrated through the print media of the country. Since independence, Senegal has had strong legal and political institutions. Its constitution from 1963 provided protection of freedom, political liberties, the rights of the trade unions, individual freedom of worship, right to property, and other economic and social rights. In 1982, Senegal ratified the African Charter on Human and Peoples' Rights.

According to a USAID report, Senegal is one of the few stable democracies in West Africa. This perception was confirmed by the 2012 elections, Senegal's third peaceful transition of power from one president to the other; two of which are considered the most democratic elections in the country. The trend of good governance creates an excellent opportunity to address some of the core challenges in Senegal. In the past decade, the country has made progress on democratic and economic governance. USAID has supported decentralization and development at the local level and promoted transparency and accountability in the institutional, electoral, and political processes in Senegal. The agency also supports social stability in the restive Casamance region, the southern part of Senegal. USAID sponsored a four-and-a-half-year project known as the Governance and Peace Program (USAID/PGP). The project is scheduled to finish in 2014 and focuses primarily on enhancing democracy, good governance, and national reconciliation (Taylor/USAID, 2014).

The goals of the project are to increase transparency and accountability, improve the fiscal decentralization efforts in the local governments, increase civil society participation in the electoral process, and support social stability in the Casamance region. In the 2012 elections, USAID/

PGP played a leading role in promoting free and credible elections by empowering the civil society to observe the elections nationwide and strengthen political party coalitions. The project also supports local communities and civil society in their efforts to resolve issues of social stability and local governance in the Casamance region. Other issues that are been supported by USAID/PGP are women's leadership and civil journalism at the community level by increasing the presence of women in local media in the Thies Diourbel regions. One of the success stories is its recently expanded pilot program in collaboration with radio Guindiku FM, which reaches over 400,000 people over a fifty-kilometer radius. The radio station is the only available source of information for the local communities (Taylor/USAID, 2014).

To support conflict mitigation and reconciliation in the Casamance region of Senegal along the border of Guinea-Bissau, a two-year peace-building project was initiated to target communities through dialogue, cultural exchange, and mediation activities. The objective of the project is to promote community reconciliation and local population participation in the Casamance conflict resolution process in southern Senegal. Due to the introduction of the new gender equality law in the Parliamentarian Assistance and Civil Engagement (PACE), 46 percent of the legislators elected in 2012 elections were women. The gender equality law provides women the opportunity to be actively involved in transforming public opinion of their roles in society. USAID also awarded an eighteen-month project to local NGOs through a consortium of local and international organizations. The goals of the project are to promote reforms that are suitable for democratic governance through capacity building for members of the National Assembly and better citizen participation in the decision-making processes in the country.[4]

---

[4] Democracy and Governance in Senegal Results of USAID's Democracy and Governance spending.

4. **[Please include the footnote number in the correct position and format as appropriate.]**Senegal has progressed significantly, both economically and politically, as a moderate, democratic, predominantly Muslim secular country in fragile West Africa.

THE WORKING OF DEMOCRACY IN NIGERIA

Overview

Before getting into the narrative of Africa's most popular country's political future, it is critical to take a brief overview of Nigeria, officially known as the Federal Republic of Nigeria. It is a federal constitutional republic comprising thirty-six states and one federal capital territory. This West African nation shares borders with the Republic of Benin in the west, Chad and Cameroon in the east, and Niger in the north. Nigeria's coastline lies on the Gulf of Guinea, which is a part of the Atlantic in the south. Its current capital city is Abuja in the center of the country, within the federal capital territory. The Nigerian people have an extensive history; archaeological evidence shows that human habitation in the area dates back to 9000 BC. This Benue-Cross River land, according to Nigerian history, is thought to be the original homeland of Bantu migrants who spread across most of southern and central Africa in the first millennium BC.

What is known today as the Federal Republic of Nigeria was originally the British protectorates of the north and south areas of the River Niger. In 1914, the two entities were formally merged for administrative reasons and became the protectorate and colony of Nigeria. In 1960, the two entities became independent Nigeria after several agitations for autonomy of various sections of the country: North, West, and Eastern Nigeria. The new independent nation was built around three regional structures dominated by three main tribes: Hausa, Igbo, and Yoruba. The new Nigerian state also adopted a British parliamentary system of government. Without consideration of the ethnic diversity of the population, including more than two hundred ethnic groups speaking more than four hundred languages, it was obvious that this dream of the independence of post-colonial Nigeria was born with many handicaps. Like most newly independent African nations in the 1960s, Nigeria was plagued by the need to bring about rapid development to satisfy many independence promises and meet the expectations of the citizens.

Without the fulfillment of these expectations, the crisis of nation building, weakened in the struggle for regional supremacy, suddenly reopened old wounds, which led to the first military coup d'état in the country in 1966.

Between 1966 and 1979, the mode of political administration in Nigeria was undemocratic, and leadership change happened through military coups, punctuated by spells of elected government that lasted for less than four years before 1991. These challenges created major obstacles to bringing about radical social change in Nigeria. However, a truly federal democracy, capable of creating conditions for effective elected leadership with good performance, did not take root until 1999, when President Olusegun Obasanjo, along with thirty-six governors of the states, came to office through the ballot box. Since then, other elections have been held in Nigeria and political power is transmitted without disruption or a complete breakdown of the social order.

THE ROLE OF CIVIL SOCIETY IN NIGERIA

Civil society has played a critical role in the political framework of Nigeria for decades. In the days of military rule, the main opposition to the military regime was the civil society, with the basic objectives to search for a more humane, responsive, and responsible social order. During that period, the only means through which citizens expressed their indignation to the misrule of the military was through the civil society. The activities of the civil society can be analyzed in the following orders:

- The immediate post-independence period between 1960 and 1965
- The periods of military rule between 1966 and 1979 and 1983 and 1999.
- The brief period of civilian democracy known as the Second Republic, between 1979 and 1983
- The permanent civilian democracy from 1999 to present

The post-independence period was too short for meaningful activities by the civil society. Due to unmet expectations after independence, the country began to experience serious political problems, starting with the treason trial of Chief Obafemi Awolowo, a Nigerian politician, statesman, and a strong advocate of independence; the Action Group crisis of 1962, and the crisis that followed the creation of Midwest Region in 1963. Other challenges include the Tiv crisis of 1964 and the Western Region crisis of 1964 and 1965, which led to the 1966 military coup that escalated into the bloody civil war that ended in 1970 (Fadakine, 1999/2012). During the period of military rule, the civil society was a remarkable force for social order, serving as the main opposition to the military misrule and the staunch defenders of citizens' rights. The civil society was at the forefront of the fight against military dictatorship with the support of the public and some segments of the international community. The work of the civil society continues under civilian democratic rule by ensuring state effectiveness, accountability, efficiency and prompt response to citizens' needs, human rights, the rule of law, and constitutionalism.

CIVIL SOCIETY AND GOOD GOVERNMENT IN NIGERIA

One would wonder what linked civil society to democracy in a country like Nigeria. To answer to this question, one has to have both radical and liberal world views. Civil society plays a critical role in ensuring that government performs its basic functions in the society. Good governance means the process of more equitably exercising political power in managing the affairs of the state. For this to happen more effectively and efficiently, civil society must check on the government. This process is particularly critical to Nigeria as the largest Black country in the world. As a regional power, Nigeria has the ability to influence the rest of West Africa in maintaining peace and security. Good governance therefore has many dimensions, including the capacity for the state to commit to transparency, accountability, the rule of law, and establishing a mechanism for conflict resolution. Good governance also means a free and fair election process that enables citizens to replace a nonperforming government that is responsible for bad governance.

Civil society has for decades been at the forefront of liberal democracy and radical social change in Nigeria. In the case of Nigeria, civil society is described as the space that exists between the federal government and individual, a space that consists of different groups and organizations, each of which is committed to upholding the values and principles needed to achieve particular objectives. This space is known in Nigerian society as the third sector, which is very distinct from the public and private sectors.

The third sector includes institutions like labor unions, professional groups, religious groups, and citizen's advocacy organizations that give voice to various sectors of the society to ensure public participation in the democratic process (DeLue, 2002, cited in Fadakinte, 2013). With all these institutions in place, why is it that democracy is not working in Nigeria and most parts of Africa? Abdukrazaq Hamzat in his (2012) excerpts, the author provides a few answers:

The author argues that Africa, and Nigeria in particular, have been unable to operate stable and successful democratic governance, consequently resulting in economic underdevelopment and mass poverty; centralization of economic and political power; corruption in various forms and manifestations, and negative historical precedent (Hamzat, 2012). Corruption and mismanagement, according to research, are two main causes of underdevelopment in Africa. These factors also act as barriers to democracy and good governance. A typical example can be seen in Nigerian oil sector; Nigeria's oil is transported to foreign countries to their economic benefit but returns to Nigeria in exploitative forms, creating scarcity and misery. The practice eventually leads to fuel subsidies, which have crippled multimillions of small and medium businesses over the years. The consequences of such policies lead to massive poverty and corruption in the sector. Similar situation can be seen elsewhere, like Liberia with Firestone (the world's largest plantation) and other resources like iron ore and timber, which are transported to foreign countries but return back to Liberia in exploitative forms.

Since the beginning of the nineteenth century, nearly all of Africa was held in structural relationship to the countries of Europe and the Americas, resulting in underdevelopment of the continent. Because of the structural relationship, African countries have been unable to practice democracy and good governance. In order to have the necessary social prerequisites for democratic governance, African countries will have to end structural relationships with the advanced countries. For the underdeveloped countries to successfully achieve democracy and good governance, they need to advocate for a level playing field to move at their own pace. This means establishing a relationship that is strictly based on mutual interest and mutual benefit. African countries must operate as independent entities, independent in governance, economic practice, policy formulation, and affiliation, in recognition of the values and principles of the African cultures.

In the Nigerian situation, the dominant class originated at independence, when the impact of colonialism created various factions in the society. The social structure was not sufficiently developed with well-defined class structures. In other words, there was no clear-cut alignment of all the class forces in Nigerian society (Fadakinte, 2002, cited in 2014). The result of the instability and fragmentation of the incohesive dominant class led to unequal distribution of resources and the struggle for economic power. The fight for economic power resulted into various factions. The unstable nature of the state makes it difficult to grow and consolidate a democratic order. These challenges make democracy a proposition that does not go beyond elections, because the dominant class equates elections to democracy and cannot distinguish civil rule from democratic rule. Because of this functionalist approach by the dominant class, there is no real assurance for good governance and democracy in Nigeria. Despite these challenges, there are other potentials in the Nigerian society, such as personal development and the working of the federal system by Nigerian standards.

With a population of 180 million, Nigeria is Africa's most populous country and the eighth most populous country in the world, according to a *New African* report (2015), making Nigeria the most populous black country in the world. Nigeria is also a regional power and listed among the top-eleven economies in the world. As a former British colony, it is a member of the Commonwealth of Nations. Nigeria also belongs to the following international organizations: African, Caribbean, and Pacific Group of States, African Development Bank, African Union, Economic Community of West African States, Food and Agriculture Organization, Group of 15, Group of 24, Group of 77, International Atomic Energy Agency, International Bank for Reconstruction and Development (World Bank), International Chamber of Commerce, International Civil Aviation Organization, International Monetary Fund, International Confederation of Free Trade Unions, International Criminal Court, Nonaligned Movement, Organization of the Islamic Conference, Organization of the Petroleum Exporting Countries, United Nations, World Trade

Organization, World Federation of Trade Unions, and several international organizations.

The Nigerian economy is one of the fastest-growing economies in the world at a rate estimated between 8 percent and 9 percent annually (IMF, 2012). With such a significant outlook, one would assume Nigeria to be one of Africa's exemplars when it comes to democracy and good governance. Ironically, Nigeria's democracy and good governance is still long in coming, according to research by Democracy Watch in Africa. In order to understand Nigeria's challenges, one must first understand the nature of the Nigerian state. To understand the issue of good governance and democracy in Nigeria, one must understand who exercises the power of the state in the first place, the same as in most African nations. This has to be the dominant class whose interests the state represents. Reportedly, 80 percent of Nigeria's energy revenues flow to the government, 16 percent covers operational costs, and the remaining 4 percent goes to investors. According to World Bank's estimate, 80 percent of the energy revenues benefit only 1 percent of the population due to corruption (Library of Congress, 2008).

Between 2003 and 2007, the Nigerian government attempted to implement an economic program known as the National Economic Empowerment Development Strategy (NEEDS). The purpose of NEEDS was to raise the standard of living through a variety of reform measures, such as macroeconomic stability, deregulation, liberalization, privatization, transparency, and accountability. The goal of NEEDS was to address deficiencies in Nigerian society, such as improving fresh water for household use and irrigation, unreliable power supplies, decaying infrastructure, impediments to private enterprise, and corruption. The hope of the government was that the program would create seven million new jobs, diversify the economy, boost non-energy exports, increase industrial capacity utilization, and improve agricultural productivity. On the state level, a related initiative has been created, known as the State Economic Empowerment Development Strategy (SEEDS). The United Nations is also sponsoring a long-term economic development program known as the National Millennium Goal for Nigeria. The UN-sponsored program covers the fifteen-year range from 2000 to 2015. Under the National Millennium Goal, Nigeria is committed to achieve a wide range of objectives, including poverty reduction, education, gender equality, health, the environment, and international development cooperation.[5]

BUHARI'S NIGERIA NOW AND THE CHALLENGES AHEAD

Nigeria's newly elected president, Muhammed Buhari, is known for his disciplinary measures. During his first administration, Buhari launched a campaign against indiscipline. Buhari's government also launched the most intense anticorruption campaign in Nigeria's history. A former military leader of the country, he once ruled Nigeria in the 1980s; but was overthrown by a military coup in August 1985 (Siollun, 2015). The new president is known for his tough stand against corruption and indiscipline. Expectations are high among Buhari's supporters and the world in general that he will deliver on some of Nigeria's most pressing issues, such as security, economic diversification, and corruption. The country also faces other problems, including gas prices in a bid to boost electricity supply (Ezeh, 2015).

In a relatively short period of time, Buhari has visited African countries, including Niger, Chad, Cameroon, Benin, and four other regional countries, in an effort to fight Boko Haram. On the foreign policy front, the new president has taken a trip to the United Sates to meet with the leaders of the West and attended the G7 meeting in Germany and the African Union summit in South Africa. The relationship between Nigeria and the United States was somewhat strange under the previous administration. It seems that Nigeria under President Buhari is in the United States' good book as evidenced by President Barack Obama's speech to the African Union in Addis Ababa, Ethiopia, making explicit references to the peaceful and free elections during Nigeria's transfer of power (Schneider, 2015).

---

[5] Fadakinte, M.M. (1999–2012), *Civil Society, Democracy and Good Governance in Nigeria:* Department of Political Science, Faculty of Social Sciences, University of Lagos, Nigeria.

8. [Please include the footnote number in the correct position and format as appropriate.]Moru, J. (2011), *Civil Society and Social Change in Nigeria:* Action Aid International, Abuja

Other challenges Buhari faces are problems of human rights abuses by the Nigerian military, according to the Amnesty International report, accusing the military of more than 7,000 deaths while in detention, and the Leahy Law, which legally prohibits the United States from providing significant military aid to militaries that violate human rights. President Buhari vowed to investigate the allegations. With less than a year in power, it remains to be seen if Buhari's reform efforts will lead to a success story in Africa's most popular country.

BENIN'S DEMOCRACY: ACHIEVEMENTS AND CHALLENGES

Overview

What is present-day Benin, was once the site of Dahomey, a prominent kingdom in West Africa in the fifteenth century. The area became a French colony in 1872 and formally achieved its independence on August 1, 1960, as the Republic of Benin. Benin shared borders with Togo, Burkina Faso, and Nigeria. Historically, most Haitians trace their ancestry to Benin. Like most of postcolonial Africa, Benin has its set of challenges after a succession of military governments that ended with the rise to power of Mathieu Kerekou, a leader who changed Benin's political landscape with the establishment of a government based on Marxist-Leninist principles. That system of government was in place until 1989, when the country moved to a representative government. Two years later, a free election was held, ushering former Prime Minister Nicephone Soglo as president, making Benin one of the first sites of the successful transfer of power from dictator to democracy in Africa. Between 1996 and 2001, former president Mathieu Kerekou was returned to power by elections, although there were allegations of some irregularities.

Since 2006, Benin's current president has been in power but not without challenges. President Yayi Boni was one of the eight African leaders invited by US President Barack Obama to attend the May 2012 G8 summit at Camp David to discuss the issue of food security. The invitation was an indication that the country is moving in the right direction, at least from the perspective of its donors in the United States and other Western countries. According to research, Benin has been an important country for donors and one of the first African countries to democratize after the Cold War; as a result, it has gained a reputation as "the laboratory of democratization in Africa" (UNU-WIDER, 2012). It has been two decades since Benin's democratic transition. During those years, the country has held five presidential elections and, at least from a procedural standpoint, its democracy appears to be consolidated (Gazibo, 2012). The role of foreign aid in Benin has now shifted from developmental purpose to specific aspects of democratic consolidation, such as free and fair elections and the promotion of civil society.

Benin received approximately $147 million in overall assistance for democracy between 2001 and 2009, amounting to 2.6 percent of its total aid commitment during that period. As a result of the commitment, donors were successful during that time in strengthening central government institutions and providing much-needed funding for consolidating the procedural aspects of the country's electoral process (Stewart, 2012). A large portion of the funding helped to develop the country's General Budget Support (GBS), which strengthened such major institutions as the executive branch of the Beninese government, the judiciary, and the civil service. The measures allowed the government to avoid a democratic breakdown. Financial and technical support from donors also helped to formulate regulations pertaining to elections and accountability. Donor support to Benin's democratic consolidation was crucial, requiring Benin to fulfill free and fair elections at regular intervals. The United States and the Netherlands in particular insisted the Ministry of Finance adequately fund the Autonomous National Election Commission (ANEC) as a funding condition.

CHALLENGES TO GOVERNANCE IN BENIN

While the presence of foreign aid has been positive, studies show it has had difficulties enhancing good governance, the rule of law, and accountability. In recent years, not all has been well in Benin. The country is losing its status as an exemplary democracy in West Africa for the following reasons:

socioeconomic turmoil, increasing corruption, and mounting opposition to the president's desire for a third term. Like Burkina Faso, Benin has had periodic general strikes threatening the school year for children. Other challenges include a series of economic scandals, including the country's own Madoff-style pyramid investment scheme that defrauded Beninese citizens of 150 million euros. More troubling is the removal of Benin from the list of countries eligible for funding by the Millennium Challenge Account (MCC) in December 2013 (Moestrup, 2014). Boni Yayi is also faced with other challenges since his election; according to Freedom House, there has been a decline in the country's freedom of the press status from "free" to "partly free."

Increasingly, there have been concerns of nepotism since the president's reelection in 2011 from surrounding himself with family members and members of the Pentecostal Church, a church that the president is a fervent devotee of. According to Freedom House, three of Boni Yayi's children served in the presidency. Other family members include his wife's older brother, who served as minister of development. The ministers of justice, labor, and environment are members of the evangelist church (Moestrup, 2014). Opponents of the president suspect that he might change the constitution to stay in office for another term. Hopefully this will not be a repeat of political developments in Burkina Faso. Benin has thus far remained on the democratic path since the country's transition to a multiparty democracy in 1990. With political courage, Benin will set an example by resisting pressure and avoiding the idea of extended presidential terms in contrast to Burkina Faso, Burundi, and the Democratic Republic of Congo (DRC).

Two areas that post major challenges are accountability and corruption. According to Freedom House, Benin is becoming a staging ground for Latin American drug dealers to get their products into Europe and Asia. Evidence shows some powerful local actors are suspected to be involved in this activity. Interventions from donor agencies come in on multiple fronts. For example, the EU promotes NGO participation in the preparation and implementation of anticorruption and accountability programs. The EU also supports programs aimed at strengthening the Beninese legal and institutional frameworks, such as the judiciary. The Netherlands runs another aid program that targets improvements in this area.

Stewart (2012), argues that there are three innovative policies to be considered. The first policy was the transformation of Benin's electoral commission to a nonpolitical body. The measure will prevent the incumbent from modifying the rules at every election. It will also discourage political parties from constantly quarreling over the election process. The second innovative policy is improving accountability and countering corruption. This measure will require the government to devote more resources to institutions that monitor the governance process. And thirdly, the need for cross-cultural rather than sector-based initiative is a major priority. Providing inclusive training with common themes would be more fruitful than providing training to individual entities separately. If all the above policies are carried out, the decline in the quality of democracy in Benin, particularly in the areas of the rule of law and corruption, can be prevented. To sustain democracy and good governance in Benin will require real political courage and commitment to reform; such measures must welcome the participation of all sectors of the society.[6]

MALI'S DEMOCRATIC BEST PRACTICE

Overview

Mali is located in central western Africa, the combined size of California and Texas (Martin, Martin, and Weil, 2002). The country's name came from the ancient Malian empire along the upper and lower Niger River, because the Niger River makes an arc through Mali from southwest to southeast. Mali has been the crossroads between northern and western Africa, according the Economic Intelligence Unit report (2002). The

---

[6] The country is rapidly losing its *status* as an exemplary *democracy* in West Africa.... At the end of December 2013, the United States removed *Benin* from the... president, third term limit on April 21, *2014* by Sophia *Moestrup*. [Please complete the sentence and cite the source.]

9. [Please include the footnote number in the correct position and format as appropriate.]Not all is well in Benin. The country is rapidly losing its status as an exemplary democracy in West Africa. Socio-economic turmoil, increasing corruption, and mounting opposition to the president's suspected desires for a third term have rocked an otherwise stable nascent democracy.

region became a French colony in the 1890s until it gained its independence from French colonial rule in 1960. It adopted a socialist economic model immediately after independence, with rural cooperatives designed to produce cotton and groundnuts as its major exports.

Mali also exports gold from a massive mine in the Kayes area, a new hope for export earnings. The gold mine is operated by a South African-Canadian consortium. In 1992 a new constitution was created after a democratic uprising, which was led by students in 1991, making Mali's first democratic transition. The country has a free press and a vibrant multiparty system of governance (Martin, P. et al, 2002). Bamako is the major city, with about one million residents, followed by three other cities: Ségou, Mopti, and Sikasso, approximately 100,000 each. The country is divided into eight regions: Kayes, Koulikoro, Ségou, Mopti, Gao, Timbau, and Bamamko.

The total population is eleven million people. According to the World Bank, the per capita income is $240, with a GDP of $2.3 billion in 2002; this statistic may be a little more in 2015 with the ongoing economic development in the country. "Mali has a human development index score of 0.38 and per capita GDP at PPP of $740. Comparing this to two of its neighbors, Côte d' Ivoire and Sengal, which have HDIs of 0.42 and per capita GDP-PPPs of $1, 600 that is more than twice as much buying power person" (Martin P. 2002; p.88). From four million in 1960 at independence, the country has experienced a rapid population growth of 3.1 percent, or 300,000 people, per year. Mali has a young population, reporting a median age of 15.9 years old.

DEMOCRATIC BEST PRACTICE:

Although Mali is generally considered one of the poorest five nations in the world, the country embraced democracy in 1991, making it a democratic role model in the Francophone region of the continent. In West Africa, Mali is one of the promising democracies (Helderman, as cited in Martin, et al, 2002). One of the strategies that have worked in Mali is its dependence on remittances, which has improved the lives of the residents by adding schools and clinics in the country. The Malian government is also open to co-development and cooperated with assisted return programs for unauthorized Malians living in France. It works with international organizations to attract educated Malians to return to the country.

With France's assistance with the co-development strategy, about five hundred unauthorized Malians living in France agreed to voluntarily return in exchange for CFA $2.5 million, equivalent to $3, 600, to open businesses in Mali. Most of the businesses were in the area of agriculture, hairdressing, importing used car parts, sewing traditional dresses, and sand dredging. The co-development strategy encountered some challenges. Malians figured prominently in the mid-1990s protests in France, when some migrants tried to avoid deportation by occupying churches. At one point in 1996, France sent a charter planes carrying deported Malians to Bamako.

The decision caused Malian President Alpha Omar Konaré to complain to the French government that "some people have been expelled with absolutely nothing; however, we cannot encourage our citizens to breach the laws of their host country" (Martin, 2002; p. 91). Those who participated in the program received weekly visits for one year from the program's office in Mali. Research shows that 80 percent of those who participated in co-development are still in business. However, returnees had difficulties obtaining bank loans for expansion because they did not have a track record or guarantees in Mali. Overall, the French model significantly helped to reintegrate some migrants who were struggling economically in France.

A United Nations program was designed to temporarily assist returning university professors. The Malian government also supported donor suggestions for economic development so that most of its citizens won't have to depend on agriculture and raising cattle in the arid regions. The strategy has resulted in competitive advantages for sustained economic growth (Martin, 2002; p.1). Research shows since September of 1999, the Malian government has promoted a policy of decentralization of power. Governing authorities who are the representatives of the central government are shared by elected mayors from 701 communes, including nineteen cities.

The second-level administrative units in the country are districts roughly equivalent to counties. About 75 percent of the citizens live in the rural areas, and 75 percent of Mali's four million economically active workers are subsistence farmers, many of whom live along the Niger River. Most of the farmers live in villages that have 150 to 600 residents. These residents primarily grow rice, wheat, and corn. Mali also grows potatoes, yams, millet, sorghum, and cassava for their own consumption. The economic and democratic reforms of Mali were rewarded with foreign aid. The United Kingdom, France, and the Netherlands are Mali's prominent donors, donating an average of $33 per person.

Due to Mali's reform efforts, donors agreed to provide the country with the equivalent of US $870 million in debt relief under the Heavily Indebted Poor Countries (HIPC) initiative. The amount was equivalent to almost half of Mali's gross domestic product. One of the major goals of the Malian government is providing access to education, which has resulted in the reduction of illiteracy in the country. Consequently, progress in reversing traditionally very low levels of primary school attendance has been seen in recent years. According to research, an estimated 60 percent of school-age Malian children are enrolled in primary schools; between 18 and 20 percent are in secondary schools, and 1.5 percent are enrolled at the universities. The enrollment of girls still lags behind that of boys, a situation that is common throughout the continent.

DEMOCRACY AND GOOD GOVERNANCE IN NAMIBIA

Overview

What is present-day Namibia, was once German South-West Africa. After World War I, the League of Nations mandated that South Africa administer the territory. It became the trusteeship of the United Nations after the League of Nations was dissolved in 1946, bringing all former German colonies in Africa under the control of the United Nations. Legal battle over the territory lasted for twenty years, until 1966, when the UN General Assembly decided to end the mandate, declaring that South Africa had no further right to administer the territory. As a result of the mandate,

South-West Africa was brought under the direct responsibility of the UN (Resolution 2145 XXI, 1966). Namibia has a diversity of origin, but the most famous peoples are San (also known as the Bushmen), considered to have been the earlier inhabitants of the region comprised of Namibia, Botswana, and South Africa. Over time, other ethnic groups, like the Bantu from the East African lakes, settled in the area that is present-day Namibia.

The first European white farmers, comprising mostly of Boers, entered the area in the seventeenth century. The Boers moved farther north, pushing the indigenous Khoisan peoples, who originally had put up fierce resistance, across the Orange River. The Basters were among the last group to settle in Namibia before the Europeans. According to research, they were the descendants of Boer men and African women, mostly Nama or Khoisan. The first European to set foot on Namibian soil was the Portuguese explorer Diogo Cao in 1485 on an exploratory mission along the west coast of Africa. In 1793 the Dutch authority in the Cape decided to take control of Walvis Bay, since the area was the only good deep-water harbor along the Skeleton Coast. The London Missionary Society followed the Dutch in 1805 and began working in Namibia, moving in a northern direction from the Cape Colony. The German Rhenish Mission Society began working in Namibia in the 1840s in collaboration with the London Missionary Society. The "scramble for Africa" by European powers to carve up the African continent did not take place until the nineteenth century, with Germany and Great Britain in the forefront of the process.

THE FIGHT FOR INDEPENDENCE IN NAMIBIA:

The struggle for independence began with the creation of the South-West Africa People's Organization (SWAPO), the military wing of the People's Liberation Army of Namibia (PLAN), which undertook guerrilla attacks on the South African forces that were infiltrating the territory. After Angola became independent in 1975, SWAPO established its bases in that country. The fight for independence brought the International Court of Justice on board, upholding UN authority over Namibia. The court then determined that South Africa's presence in Namibia was illegal, demanding the withdrawal of South Africa's administration from Namibia immediately. In 1977, the Western Contact Group (WCG) was founded. It launched a joint diplomatic effort to bring an acceptable international transition to independence for Namibia. The five WCG countries were United Kingdom, Canada, France, West Germany, and the United States. The efforts of WCG led to the adoption of the 1978 Security Council Resolution 435 to settle the Namibian problem. After a lengthy consultation with South Africa, and the frontline states of Angola, Botswana, Mozambique, Tanzania, Zambia, and Zimbabwe, SWAPO, the United Nations, and Western Contact Group, a settlement proposal was reached.

After many consultations, Namibia finally became independent on March 21, 1990. The ceremony was attended by several international representatives, including the main players, including UN Secretary General Javier Perez de Cuellar and then-president of South Africa F. W. de Klerk, who jointly conferred formal independence for Namibia. San Nujoma, president of SWAPO, was sworn in as the first president of Namibia. At the ceremony was Nelson Mandela, who had been released from prison shortly beforehand after twenty-seven years, and representatives from 147 countries, including twenty heads of state. Since independence, Namibia has successfully completed the transition from white minority Apartheid rule to a democratic society. A multiparty democracy was introduced and has been maintained, with local, regional, and national elections held regularly. According to Africa Democracy Watch, there are several active political groups represented in the National Assembly, although SWAPO, the ruling party, has continued to win every election since independence.

Namibia is considered one of Africa's most stable democracies since independence. In 1994, San Nujoma was reelected with 76.34 percent of the votes in the presidential election. In 1998, with one year until the next scheduled presidential elections, SWAPO amended the constitution to allow three terms instead of two. The decision was intended to enable San Nujoma to participate in the election; he had already served the two terms that the constitution allowed. They were able to make a constitution amendment because SWAPO had two-thirds majorities in both the National Assembly of Namibia and the National Council, which was the minimum needed to amend the constitution. San Nujoma was reelected as president in 1999, winning with 76.82 percent in an election that had a 62.1 percent turnout rate. San Nujoma chose not to run for the presidency again, although a constitutional amendment would have allowed him to run for a fourth term. The transition from the fifteen-year rule of President San Nujoma to his successor, Hifikepunye Pohamba, in 2005 went smoothly, according to election results. The Namibian government has promoted a policy of national reconciliation and issued an amnesty for those who fought on either side during the liberation war.

THE STATE OF NAMIBIAN DEMOCRACY

Namibia is now widely considered by the international community as an example of successful democratic regime transition, because the country's democratic institutions are generally stable, compared to neighboring states like Angola and South Africa or more distant trouble spots like Cambodia, Nicaragua, Egypt, and other struggling democracies around the world. Namibia has made the most successful and peaceful transition to an electoral democratic process (Lindeke, 1995). What was once considered a model transition now looks more like an exception to post–Cold War pattern. Despite the positive and favorable judgments of Namibia's democratic process, there is caution about the common problems of Africa's earlier experiences with democratization. One of those problems has to do with the issue of "state softness," which affects the country's politics and economic development.

State softness primarily has to do with the condition in which the institutions of the state have limited autonomy when it comes to the combined influences of external forces and the role of civil society. This limited autonomy affects the capacity and effectiveness of a state's ability to carry out defined and normal function. There are three aspects of state softness that have become problematic for African countries. The first aspect is that African states are dominated by outside forces that mobilize greater resources and have greater control over their environment. A few examples of the outside forces include former colonial governments, transnational corporations, and multilateral agencies such as the World Bank and the International Monetary Fund. Added to the forces are the dominance of the world culture of capitalism, which includes language, fashion, information, and the patterns of assumption that tend to limit the ability of states to function. The second aspect of softness is state weakness, which began after independence from colonial rule due to the limited skills and experience of African citizens. The third softness is the fact that African states are relatively weak and vulnerable to infiltration and manipulation from elements of civil society, such as traditional ethnic interests, family and language attachments, and class interests of the ruling elites. All these forces serve as barriers to the democratic process in Namibia and the rest of Africa in general.

Namibia also encountered external domination after independence from the impact of trade and investments from South Africa. Namibia, like other African countries that became independent some thirty years ago, faces difficult choices and demanding tasks for achieving development and pursuing a democratic path. Like the rest of Southern Africa, Namibia's economy was established during years of colonial domination. In many countries, the settlers created a large pool of cheap labor for the dominant economic enterprises, mostly in the mining and agriculture sectors, with very little manufacturing capacity. Despite all these weaknesses, Namibian democratic and economic transformations continue to make progress.

According to UNDP's review in 2004, there were no serious setbacks to report in the process of reform. The political highlight of the evaluation showed that voters in Namibia have gone to the polls three times in presidential, parliamentary, and regional elections. The review demonstrated that after almost fifteen years of independence, all elections took place with remarkable political routine, with minor exceptions. Namibia has a universal franchise; its citizens have the right to vote and to stand for election at the national, regional, and municipal levels. The review showed that elections were free and fair for the fourth time with 85 percent turnout rates for the national elections and 54 percent for the regional elections. Elections, monitored by an independent election commission, met international standards. Opposition parties were able to exercise freedom of opinion and freedom of assembly, although there were some complaints about restrictions and obstacles in the SWAPO strongholds in the northern part of the country.

Due to the dominance of SWAPO, the influence of the opposition and the constitutional checks and balances function to a limited extent. Since independence, SWAPO has enjoyed a three-quarter majority in parliament and the support of the dominant Ovambo ethnic group, the largest ethnic group in Namibia. Despite SWAPO's dominant influence, the Namibian parliament meets regularly, creating an avenue for open and critical discussion where the opposition parties can express their opinions without restriction or hindrance. Such practice is carried out at regional and municipal councils. On the rule of law, the courts are independent, and judges and officials of the court act in accordance with the constitution. However, in recent years, some reservations have been expressed about political partiality in the appointment of judges, although these reservations have not been substantiated. The Namibian constitution attaches great emphasis to division of powers and responsibilities between the executive, legislative, and judicial branches of government.

On the socioeconomic development front among countries in southern Africa, Namibia has a fairly high level of development, with a per capita income of $1,870, which can be translated to the international equivalent of about $6, 620 in terms of purchasing power parity. Consequently, Namibia is considered a lower-middle-income Country by Western standards, not a low-income country. According to a UNDP review, such global indicators conceal striking differences in income and social disparities (UNDP, 2003). According to the key measures of the World Bank, the country's macroeconomic position was relatively stable during the period of the review. Due to its mineral wealth and its favorable position between Angola and South Africa, two powerful economic partners, Namibia has considerable growth potential in the field of tourism. Compared to other countries in southern Africa, Namibia's political leadership at the time of independence had a good fortune. As a result, Namibia started with relatively high levels of economic and social development. [7]

---

[7] William A. Lindeke, "Soft State, Hard Choices." *Studies in Comparative International Development: Democratization in Namibia.* Spring 1995, Vol. 30, No. 1, 3–29–ISSN: 0039-3606 (Print) 1936-6167

THE DEMOCRATIC REPUBLIC OF CONGO (DRC)

When it comes to mineral resources, the Democratic Republic of Congo is one of the richest countries in Africa and among the wealthiest in the world. Its rich mineral resources include strategic minerals such as diamonds and cotton; its biodiversity is almost unparalleled in the world. At the same time, its water resources extend over three million square miles of the Congo River basin, one of the longest rivers in the world. It is unfortunate to note that with all these resources, not much has been used for the benefit of the Congolese people. Congo, like the rest of the Great Lakes region, has had a turbulent colonial and postcolonial history. Historically, the territory was acquired as the personal property of King Leopold II of Belgium, also called the Congo Free State, as it was commonly known then, ironically given freedom to Western capital, and death and enslavement to the indigenous population during colonial periods. Millions of people died in genocidal proportions in order to supply labor to the plantations. Villages were exterminated or gotten rid of completely, bodies mutilated, and diseases spread in epidemic proportions (Hochschild, 1998).

THE ORIGINS OF THE KATANGA STATE

The Katanga province, as it is known today, was a breakaway state that separated itself from the newly independent Democratic Republic of Congo and proclaimed it to the world on July 11, 1960. The revolt was against the new government of Patrick Lumumba, a democratically elected prime minister. In July 1960, Katanga declared its independence under Moise Tshombe, who was the leader of the CONAKAT party. Ironically, the new Katanga government did not enjoy the full support it needed from the people throughout the province, especially in the northern part, known as Balubaareas. Congo's transition to an independent state was marred by the Belgian colonial support for Kantanga secessionists and motivated by Cold War rivalry, which resulted in the brutal murder of the country's democratically elected prime minister, Patrick Lumumba, the first prime minister of Congo, and his subsequent replacement by Joseph Mobutu, a military person. Also supporting the Katanga independence were Belgian business interests and over 6,000 Belgian troops. Moise Tshombe, the leader of the CONAKAT party and the breakaway state, was known to be allied with the Belgian industrial companies in charge of the rich resources of copper, gold, and uranium. Katanga was and still is one of the richest and most developed areas of the Congo.

The Congolese government would lose a large part of its mineral assets and consequently government income without the resources from the Katanga province. The Katanga situation is like the Biafra conflict in Nigeria in 1967, which also took the lives of thousands of people. The views of the international community and the Congolese central government were an attempt to create a Belgian-controlled puppet state for the benefit of the mining interests. The Katanga province accounted for nearly 50 percent of Congolese revenues and was prepared to become an independent and autonomous state. Tshombe, the leader of the breakaway state, and his officials at the time believed their actions to secede from the Democratic Republic of Congo would avoid chaos and because the current regime under Prime Minister Patrice Lumuba was influenced by communism. The Katanga government under Moise Tshombe wanted to appeal to Belgian for military aid and to the United States for recognition for his cause, because they shared common concerns about the exploitation of the Congo crisis by the Soviet Union. According to experts, not even Belgium was in full support of the new state, despite providing it with military assistance. Initially, the Tshombe government organized a military force, designating the Katanga Gendarmerie, raised from regular Belgian officers and subsequently by European mercenaries recruited from various European countries in support of the effort.

The myth among the United Nations during the 1961 Katanga crisis was that it was an expression of indigenous nationalist sentiment. But that myth was proven to be wrong as evidenced by the opposition of the leaders from the northern districts of the province, who were not consulted on the matter. Secession leader Moise Tshombe strategically aligned himself with the white European-descended settler elite, because they possessed much needed professional skills, and an exodus of such people in the face of communist rule would likely prove fatal to their homeland's industry. The decision by Katanga to unilaterally declare its independence drew the attention of the United Nations secretary general with a telegram from

Prime Minister Patrice Lumumba, insisting the UN do something about Belgian military aggression in his country and their overt backing of the Katanga secession. Among the members of the United Nations, there were mixed feelings toward Katanga, with Britain and France remaining neutral and later not supporting peacekeeping in Congo. Britain had initially provided general assistance to UN troops but refused to cooperate with subsequent efforts to deal with Tshombe's rebellious regime. Portugal and the Union of South Africa were openly in opposition to the operation from its very beginning and maintained consistent opposition against any interference with a Katanga state (Geral-Libois, 1993).

The conflict continued with a poorly organized incursion by the Congolese government into Katanga with ANC soldiers using a motley assortment of Soviet military vehicles. Consequently, the attackers, who according to historical account were literally raping and murdering their way through the countryside, were driven off by the European-officered Katanga Army. The incident worsened relations between the two governments. Fighting was sporadic for the next two years. Patrice Lumumba was eventually replaced in a military coup by Joseph Mobutu. On January 17, 1961, Lumumba was sent to Elisabethville and subsequently tortured and executed shortly after his arrival in the province. The death of Lumumba forced the United Nations Security Council to adopt Resolution 161, which authorized all appropriate measures to prevent the occurrence of civil war. The UN Security Council included the use of force, if necessary, as a last resort. In addition to the use of force, the resolution demanded the expulsion of all Belgian troops and foreign mercenaries from the Congo. During a period of six months, the United Nations undertook no major military operations, instead concentrating their efforts on a few rounds of political negotiations. The crisis continued with an increased presence of an authorized Security Council in Elisabethville. By mid-1961, presidential security forces had killed 7,000 Balubas, an indigenous tribal group from Katanga province. The increased number of peacekeepers in the province further enraged the Baluba people, who viewed the United Nations as an unwanted intruder, and they began to attack both the Katangan government forces and the UN soldiers with little discrimination.

The Congolese crisis brought in a sizable force of close to five hundred British, Zimbabwean (formerly Rhodesian), French, and South African irregulars. Many of the mercenaries were given command assignments in the Gendarmes, while others formed a pro-Tshombe unit known as the International Company, mostly composed of white South African fighters. Most notable among the mercenaries were the professional career soldiers who had fought in the Algerian war. Serious fighting broke out again as President Tshombe began to incite both Katanga civilians and white mercenaries to attack United Nations forces after the UNUC dispatched elements of the nearly 5,000-strong Ninety-Ninth Infantry Brigade into the capital. As the fighting escalated, UN the secretary general criticized Belgian mercenaries for their service in Katanga and condemned Tshombe for turning the Katangan public against the United Nations forces. Three days later, more fighting broke out when South African Gendarmes assaulted Kabalo, a Baluba town in the northern part of Katanga, and engaged the Ethiopian peacekeepers who were stationed there. It was not until April 30, 1961, that the state of Katanga agreed to cease hostilities.

In June, President Moise Tshombe was arrested after attending the Coquilhatville Conference of Congolese Leaders. His arrest was carried out by President Joseph Mobutu's police force the day he was about to board a plane to go back to Katanga. Tshombe was held under house arrest and charged with inciting revolt against the Congolese government, the illegal seizure of arms and aircraft, and printing counterfeit money by issuing a Katangan currency. As a condition for his release, Tshombe subsequently signed a pledge to reunite Katanga with the rest of the nation. He broke his commitment by openly declaring in a speech later that month that he would defend Katanga's rights as a sovereign state, and he vowed to do everything to maintain the status quo even in the face of all opposition (Wikipedia, 2002). The breakaway Katanga crisis lasted from 1960 to 1963.

Joseph Mobutu, the lifelong leader of the Democratic Republic of Congo, later turned out to be tyrannical dictator, silencing the voice of the Congolese people. Mobutu cleverly and effectively used the Cold War to hold onto power for many years, with Western complicity. Mobutu renamed the country Zaire and became the staging post for US anti-communist wars, along with Liberia in West Africa, where the Voice of America (VOA) was relayed to the rest of the continent. Mobutu marginalized the masses of his people with resource exploitation, corporate concessions led to the vast wealth of the country through the institution of contrast with corrupt state institutions that benefits very few.

Under the dictatorship of Mobutu Sese Seko from 1956 to 1997, Zaire did not have a fully integrated, controlled political system. During the post–Cold War era, which began in 1996, Congolese rebels known as the Alliance des Forces Democratiques pour la Liberation de Congo, which was backed by Rwanda and Uganda, became a center of focus. Laurent-Desire Kabila, who replaced Mobutu, was unable to end the corrupt practices from the past regime, consequently escalating the situation in Zaire.

In 1998, more trouble led by the Rassemblement Conolais pour la Democratie, an anti-Mobutuism movement supported by Rwanda and Uganda, forced Kabila to call on his southern African neighbors Angola, Namibia, and Zimbabwe for military support. The crisis involved seven countries and ten rebel movements. According to a report by the United Nations on the illegal exploitation of Congolese primary resources, Kabila used the country's extensive resources of strategic minerals to obtain military assistance and training. The report alleged that Kabila subsidized the costs of the allies' intervention by giving concessions to Zimbabwean and Namibian companies. Three neighboring countries also exploited the conflict for their own security interests.

These countries export timber and strategic minerals around the world, and because of the conflict, their production has risen dramatically in recent years. How has globalization impacted the Great Lakes region with its history of violence, genocide, forced labor, and displacement? The region has been negatively impacted with the impoverishment of the people by the global economy for as far back as the colonial period, including the nature of politics, the dependence of these economies on resource extraction, a declining life expectancy since the 1970s. About $15 billion in international debt has been accrued by the affected countries. Years of civil war have compounded the issue of impoverishment; the fighting and displacement of the population have disrupted their livelihoods. According to a United Nations report, resource extraction and serving international markets, among others, are seen as major contributing factors to the continued conflict in the Democratic Republic of Congo and Rwanda.

MUSIC

The Democratic Republic of Congo is also known for its musical gifts on the continent, one of the best in Africa. Congolese music attracts most of sub-Sahara Africa and beyond. The music of the Democratic Republic of Congo has different forms. Outside of Africa and on the continent, most music from the DRC is called *soukous*, due to the style of dance popularly known in the late 1960s. The terms *rumba* or *rock-rumba* are also used generically to refer to Congolese music, though neither is precise nor an accurate description. According to Congolese experts interviewed, people from the Congo have no term for their own music, per se, although *muzikinabiso*, or "our music," was used until the late 1970s. Now the most common name is *ndule*, which means "music" in the Lingal language. Most songs from the Democratic Republic of Congo are sung in Lingala. Since the colonial period, Kinshasa, the Congolese capital, has been one of the primary centers of musical innovation in Africa, alongside Nairobi, Kenya, Lagos, Nigeria, Johannesburg (South Africa), and Abidjan in the Ivory Coast, when it comes to musical influence in Africa.

As in most of Africa, the DRC is comprised of territories controlled by many different ethnic groups, many of which have little in common with each other. Each of these ethnic groups maintain their own traditional folk music. Until the 1940s, Pan-Congolese musical identity was little known. Rumba is a fusion of Latin and African musical styles that came from the island of Cuba. Creatively, the Congolese musicians appropriated rumba and adapted its characteristics for their own instruments and tastes. Some popular Congolese musicians include Feruzi, who is said to have popularized rumba during the 1930s. Early Congolese musicians include Zachery Elenga, Antoine Wendo Kolosory, and, most influentially, Jean Bosco Mwenda. In 1953, the Congolese musical scene began to differentiate itself with the formation of African Jazz, led by Joseph "Grand Kalle" Kabasele, the first full-time orchestra to record and perform, and the debut of fifteen-year-old guitarist Franccois Luuambo Makiadi (a.k.a. Franco). Both of them would go on to become some of the earliest Congolese musical stars. African Jazz, which includes Kabasele, sometimes referred to as the "father of modern Congolese music," as well as legendary Cameroonian saxophonist and keyboardist Manu Dibango, became some of the well-known groups in Africa. One of their pieces in the 1960s known as

"Independent Cha Cha," which celebrated Congo's independence, became an anthem for most Africans across the continent, especially sub-Sahara Africa (French National Library, 2010).

Between the 1930s and 1970s was the period of big bands. Especially in the 1950s, Kinshasa became a cultural conduit for many African musicians moving back and forth, including some of the most famous names in African music, like Nino Malapet and founder of OK Jazz Jean Serge Essous. Both OK Jazz and African Jazz continued performing throughout the decades until the break-up of African Jazz in the mid-1960s. Tabu Ley Rochereau and Dr. Nico then formed African Fiesta, which incorporated new innovations throughout the continent of Africa, as well as American and British soul, rock, and country music. Many of the most influential musicians in Congo's history emerged from one or more of these big bands, including the most legendary Sam Mangwana, Ndombe Opetum, Vicky Longomba, Dizzy Madjeku, and Kiamanguana Verckys.

Sam Mangwana was the most popular of these *susolo* performers, giving him a royal fan base even while switching from Vox Africa and Festival des Marquisards to Africa, followed by OK Jazz and a return to Africa before setting up a West African group called the African All Stars. Mose Fan Fan of OK Jazz also became influential, bringing the Congolese rumba to East Africa, especially the nation of Kenya, after moving there in 1974 with Somo Somo. The rumba music spread throughout the rest of Africa, with Brazzaville's Pamelo Mounk'a and Tchico Thicaya moving to Abidjan, the Ivory Coast, and Ryco Jazz taking the Congolese sound to the French Antilles. Some of the most influential groups between 1970s and 1990s include Stukas and Zaiko Lango Langa. Other legendary Congolese musicians were Bella Bella, Shama Shama, and Lipua Liua, while Kiamanguana Verkys went on to promote a rougher garage-like musical sound that launched the careers of Pepe Kalle and Kanda Bongo Man, among others.

REFORMING RWANDA'S ECONOMY

After a brutal civil war that claimed the lives of nearly 800,000 innocent civilians between 1990 and 1994, the country is now picking itself up by attracting investment opportunities. Recent events in Rwanda demonstrate how far the country has come economically since the 1990 to 1994 events and the repercussions that caused a spillover war in neighboring eastern Congo for eight years. It also highlights how far the country still has to go in reforming its democracy. For the purpose of this book, the focus will be a look at the extremely optimistic goals of the Rwandan economy (Ford, 2010). The country has shown a good track record of promoting economic growth and attracting foreign investment. Rwanda is turning itself into one of the darlings of the donor community. On the other hand, a genuine political debate is yet to take root. There is criticism of a lack of political freedom in the country in recent years. Political opponents have criticized current president Paul Kagame and his party for harassing opponents and their domination of the political system, which opponents claim was not healthy for a multiparty democracy, a charge President Kagame denies.

The European Union praised the calm atmosphere and high voter turnout at the polls but at the same time expressed concern over pre-election political violence. The presidential elections attracted a massive 93 percent of the popular vote in favor of President Paul Kagame, out of sight of his nearest opponent, Jean Damascene Ntawukuliryayo of the Social Democratic Party, with 5 percent of the vote. Despite criticism from opponents, the National Election Commission executive secretary commented, "We are very happy with the conduct of the electoral process, from the campaign to the voting itself. We did not get reports of intimidation from anywhere" (Ford, 2010). The optimism in Rwanda is based on the fact that the president and his coalition government continue to be determined to proceed with the country's economic reform program. The goal of the Rwandan government is to transform Rwanda into a middle-income nation. The government asserts that Kigali hopes to increase electricity access by 3 percent, use of clean water by 100 percent, and energy production from the current 70 to 1,000 milliwatts.

Another goal is to increase industrial production by 12 percent annually, which in turn will lead to a 20 percent increase in the gross domestic product (GDP), reducing the number of Rwandans who earn $1 a day to 30 percent of the total population. Regionally, other East African states are also seeking to rapidly develop their own power sectors in the area. Arguably, it is a fact that much economic progress that has been made in a relatively in a short period of time. The rate of economic growth stands at 9.4 percent annually. Kigali, the capital, created an attractive investment environment over the past decade. For example, corporate tax has been reduced to a lower rate, cut from 28 percent to 20 percent. According to a 2011 survey by the World Bank, Rwanda is the best country in East Africa for doing business. Rwanda was ranked among the top ten reformers out of the 183 countries surveyed, demonstrating how easy it is for local people to set up and manage businesses. On average it takes forty-five days to start a business in Africa, but in Rwanda it now takes just three days on average, because there are two simple procedures to complete. Rwanda has also been praised for reducing the level of bureaucratic attachment to cross-border trade.

Regional integration is having a positive impact on border controls and trade in East African. The policy is helping to boost the economy in two ways: first, by harmonizing trade rules and taxes within the East African Community (EAC) and providing an opportunity for Rwandan companies to market their goods to other EAC member states. It also helps to increase investment in the country by companies based in the region. As far as the profitability of Rwandan businesses, that remains to be seen, given the competitive nature of the region. But the development of a single-market policy will certainly create a larger regional economy. Another policy initiated by the government in 2008 was the decision to switch the educational system from French to English. The policy will ease integration with other EAC member states in the region where English is dominant. Regional integration will help to boost East Africa's already sizable tourism industry, allowing visitors of member states to spend part of their holiday in a neighboring country. Many tourists who travel to East Africa are attracted to Kenya and Tanzania because of the spectacular wildlife. Tour operators could decide to speed up to a week in Rwanda in an attempt to view other wildlife, if there were no additional visa requirement for their guests.

Part of the economic growth is the result of the booming telecom industry in the country. According to the Rwandan Utilities and Regulatory Agency, the mobile telecom market has been growing by 14 percent annually, an indication of the growth of the industry. More investment has also been attracted into the banking industry. The Kenyan banking industry has already set up a branch network in Rwanda and is opening branches in the country. The Bank of Rwanda plans to increase the number of ATM cards in use from 35,000 to 500,000; presumably that number may already have increased.

THE ROLE OF WOMEN IN RWANDA

According to the United Nations Commission on the Status of Women, developing countries, especially countries that are emerging from armed conflicts, are more successful at integrating women into the political process than most Western democracies. Women have taken impressive strides in just a few years to gain positions compared to their Western counterparts. Most Western democracies have struggled to achieve the integration of women after decades of conflict and backlash. On the African continent, women in Rwanda, Burundi, and Liberia (countries with a history of civil conflict) have made impressive marks in obtaining positions of power. Evidently, Rwanda leads the world, with 48.8 percent of women in parliament. In 2003 women were overwhelmingly elected to the lower house in Rwanda, putting the country in the top position in the world, compared to industrialized countries like the United States, which ranks sixty-ninth in the world with 15 percent female representation in the US Congress and 22 percent in its state legislatures. Despite these recent gains in positions of power, women of all nations, according to UN reports, still comprised 16.4 percent of all legislators in upper and lower parliaments (Gurirab, 2010).

It is not only the numerical increase of women parliamentarians that has led to a successful outcome in Rwanda but also the presence of women's activists and the initiation of a highly developed consultative policy model. There is a Rwanda Women Parliamentarians Forum, a cross-party political caucus that coordinates women's agendas in the country. Since 2003, the caucus has been working to enhance gender equality within the Rwandan parliament. The caucus's primary purpose is to initiate gender-sensitive laws, as well as improving gender-based governmental oversight. One of its major achievements was the introduction of the 2006 landmark bill to combat gender-based violence. Support also came from the leadership of Rwandan women parliamentarians and the civil society. The process, which lasted more than two years, was highly participatory, involving all the stakeholders that have interests in the laws. The women's forum also collaborated closely with men, involving them in every stage of the policy-making process. Interestingly, when the bill was introduced in parliament, it was gender sensitive, with four men and four women serving as sponsors (Gurirab, p. 36).

THE SIERRA LEONE EXPERIENCE: GOOD GOVERNANCE, DEMOCRATIC REFORM AND ACCOUNTABILITY

After period of civil war, Sierra Leone has taken the path of good governance as a central issue in the quest for the establishment and sustenance of democracy and growth-oriented in the country. The Sierra Leone's experience also involves the management of public affairs in a manner that is more participatory and responsive to the needs of the people. The reform effort includes an impartial, transparent and effective management of resources intended to benefit all Sierra Leoneans. In the past, bad governance has been the cause of disparity between Sierra Leone's potential for socio-economic and political development. The experience may also be rule of wakening from the brutal civil war; which brought an awareness to consider decision-making that works. Sierra Leone like its neighbor Liberia has learned from the impact of civil war due to undemocratic history of the state and concept of rule and law. In order to have a sustainable, stable democracy and good governance, it became increasingly critical for the country to pay close attention to proper record keeping.

While other African countries may consider different issues as national priority, proper record keeping had a continuing primary values in Sierra Leone; as evident by the people's rights and obligations. John Abdul Kargbo has written extensively on the topic and discussed the relationship between good governance and proper record keeping as a means for sustainable development in Sierra Leone. Kargbo, (2000) provided three components of good governance: the first form of good governance is political authority that exists in the country such as parliamentary authority, military authority, democratic, and authoritative rule. The second form of good governance is through the exercise of authority in the management of economic and social resources. Such an exercise and management depends on the component of governance. The third form of good governance is the ability for government to discharge its functions effectively and equally through the design, formulation and implementation of sound policies and programs (p. 2). Synthesizing Kargbo's assertion, good governance is the exercise of political, economic, and administrative authority in the management of national affairs.

Not too many African nations have placed more emphasis on proper record keeping as a fundamental tool for good governance as Sierra Leone has done. There is empirical evidence that supports that where information is properly recorded, policy decisions have been made in a timely faction to meet the changing social environment and global challenges of the 21st century. An improper record keeping lead to institutional barrier and legal reforms and eventually disguising corruption, delay justice, prolongs poverty and retards socio-economic growth (Kargbo, 2000). In Sierra Leone, proper record keeping is increasingly becoming a crucial instrument in reforming the public sector and civil service machinery of the country. In the past the government has experienced major problems in obtaining accurate statistics about the sizes and cost running civil service. A few examples are the Ministry of Social Welfare and Rural Development, Gender and Children Affairs, Development and Economic Planning and Finance, there have been problems with duplication and responsibilities due to improper record keeping (p. 4).

The current political, economic and social development of Sierra Leone since the ten years of civil war has supported by an organized record keeping system in the government. On the political front, the work of the state is being primarily defined with the introduction of democratic governance and the formation of a number of civil society organizations such as youth organizations, women's and children's rights, and advocacy of human rights. The efforts for good governance also put demands on the government by citizens for transparency and accountability. In the new reform environment, citizens and their leaders are expected to be aware that information plays a critical role in building relationships with citizens based on trust, integrity and the provision of quality service by the government. It is also expected for citizens and their leaders to understand the various needs of citizens and other stakeholders and respond to those needs with proper information that is complete, relevant, timely, accessible and well organized.

In a visit to Sierra Leone in 2009 by former British Prime Minister Tony Blair, the prime minister was quoted that "Sierra Leone was now on the most positive path that he had ever seen" according to the Harvard International Review. This optimism by Tony Blair in addition to the new administration of President Ernest Bai Koroma and the economic possibilities offered by the country's tourism industry has given real chance of making Sierra Leone one of Africa's success stories. Much credit is given to the Ernest Bai Koroma and his ruling party, the All People's Congress for the country's progress. The current president promised to run the government like a business and followed through on his oath. To fulfill his promise, the president has instituted a policy requiring performance contract for cabinet ministers. The goal of the contracts is to decrease corruption and levity in government by incentivizing efficiency and good performance. If the method works, the Koroma's government will potentially revolutionize approaches to good governance across the continent.

One of the major decisions by Mr. Koroma is the appointment of a woman: Umu Hawa Tejan-Jalloh to a powerful role of Chief Justice as head of Sierra Leone judiciary. With such appointment, Tejan-Jalloh becomes the third in Africa to run a powerful branch of government. Her appointment was an indication of a society-wide commitment by President Koroma's government to equal women participation; placing Sierra Leone on the vanguard of sub-Sahara African nations on the issues of gender equality. Tejan-Jalloh served as Sierra Leone's Chief Justice from 2008 to 2016. Abdulai Hamid Charm is the current Chief Justice of Sierra Leone; who succeeded Tejan-Jallohin January, 2016. Another dramatic change is Mr. Koroma's determination to win Sierra Leone off of its dependence from foreign aid; especially from British aid, its former colonial power. The long term goal of the president is to eventually shift his country's socialist economy to a more free-market economy system. Revitalizing the country's tourism industry is another major initiative by the government. In the

1970s and 1980s, Sierra Leone was a major travel destination. Due to the civil war, the industry was severely destroyed.

Today, Sierra Leone's neighbor, the Gambian tourism industry welcomes over 100,000 visitors every year. Comparing to Sierra Leone, its neighbor, which currently attracts only 4,000 tourists per year; but with an enthusiastic and aggressive government effort, there is no doubt that Sierra Leone can once again become one of world's most sought-after travel spots. The country is rich with natural harbor, unspoiled beaches, mountains, rich cultural history, and diverse flora and fauna (Harvard International Review, 2009: p. 9). In his one year anniversary in office, Koroma has lots of reasons to be happy. In less than two years in office, the Koroma's government was able to restore electricity to the capital city of Freetown and its environs. Such a move in a very short time created a glowing praise from the people. The government considered the energy sector as a major priority. The Sierra Leonean government has also introduced reforms in the economy and the banking and financial sectors. The government's reform efforts have resulted in the arrival of major foreign banks in the country.

One of the most radical policies in the public sector is its eradication of thousands of ghost workers off public payroll, saving taxpayers million of "Leone" (the Sierra Leonean currency). So far the government has committed itself to create an environment for the private sector to thrive with necessary legislation and infrastructure are being put in place to accommodate the initiative. Sierra Leone can also celebrate 12 years of continuous democracy since the brutal civil war. The Koroma's government is committed to freedom of the press, transparency and respect for the rule of law. Such radical reform efforts by Sierra Leone serve as motivation for its neighbors in the region; especially Liberia that shared similar culture, social and political histories.

CHALLENGES:

With all of the success stories in Sierra Leone, there are some downside issues. Like most African nations, unemployment and poverty in the country are still high according to studies by democracy watch report.

These issues of unemployment and poverty have resulted in large number of street traders and burglaries. There are also increasing lawlessness in certain section of the society and in some state agencies such as the police force. For a country coming out of the brutal war, reforming the civil order is a work in progress and does not happen overnight. However, there is hope by many in the country with four more years in the Koroma's administration that his government will fully deliver in addressing the needs of its citizens; especially the issues of unemployment and poverty.

The decision to reform the country whether in Sierra Leone or any other African nation will require a total involvement of all; both the government, civil society, and the private sectors. Unfortunately in most African countries, the government is the highest employer. This is another challenge most developing countries are faced with; doing everything for the people. The gospel that should be preached is total involvement for higher heights come through self help; as the late President William Tolbert used to advocate in Liberia; where everyone is doing something in their respective community to develop the country. That is the challenge in the 21st century and a primary challenge for the people of Africa. A challenge that Sierra Leone is not an exception of; giving the commonality of issues across the continent.

CHAPTER SEVEN

————◦———⌒————◦————

HYBRID REGIMES OR
HESITANT REFORMERS

DEMOCRATIC PRACTICE IN MOZAMBIQUE

Overview

The history of Mozambique is traced by to the legendary Vasco da Gama on his epic expedition to find a sea route to India in 1498. Vasco de Gama and his crew of sailors came ashore somewhere in the region that is now known as Inhambane Province, a southern coastal area of Mozambique. Captain Vasco de Gama intended to stop and stock up on supplies, rest, and mend the sails battered by winds on the long voyage that spanned two oceans. Instead of being greeted by war drums, spears, and arrows landing against the hulls of his caravels, the expedition was received by the natives with courtesy. The captain made a tribute to the hospitality and kindness of the Inhambane people for their unexpected courtesy. There is a certain region of southern Mozambique to this day that is affectionately known as "the land of the kind people." Historians recorded that the Portuguese were not the first non-African people to come in contact with the inhabitants of the region.

Records also indicate the presence of Arabs, Persians, and even Chinese who traded with the natives along the Indian Ocean for many centuries (Gumende,

2010). However, Portugal was one of the oldest colonial powers in Africa, with a history of presence in African territories, such as the present-day independent states of Angola, Mozambique, Cape Verde, Guinea-Bissau, and Sao Tomé and Principe. However, the presence of the Portuguese in Mozambique was limited to forts and trading ports along the coast and the Zambezi River until the late nineteenth century. Over time the concession developed into independent micro-political areas, with ruling families of mixed Afro-Indian-Portuguese descent and thoroughly Africanized cultures. At the end of the century, the Portuguese managed to conquer most of present-day Mozambique. Between 1929 and 1941, the tradition of indirect administration was carried out by international concession companies. These international concession companies were primarily in charge of most of the territory in Mozambique. The country was eventually brought under a unified system of colonial administration (Hall and Young, 1997, cited by Virtanen in 2010).

Mozambique is often referred to as a "success story" because it serves as a model for other African countries to follow, especially the frontline states in southern Africa. In Witney Schneidman's book *Engaging Africa: Washington and the Fall of Portugal's Colonial Empire*, the author writes that nearly thirty years after Mozambique's independence, the country had established an enduring reputation for good governance and sound economic management, making Mozambique one of Africa's more successful democracies (Schneidman, 2004, cited in *Hispanic Research Journal*, 2010). Such a tribute is not only a positive reassurance for a country that has suffered immensely in its thirty-five-year history since independence but also for a continent that has been blemished by negative views of its political, social, and economic conduct and prospects.

Much progress has been made during those thirty-five years of existence. To understand the enormous progress, one has to comprehend Mozambique's eventful historical trajectory from colonial times to its liberation struggles to independence and from the destabilization of war to peace in order to put the recent achievements in development into their proper context. Less than twenty years ago, according to research, Mozambique was considered a "failed state" due to war.

In 1962, the Front for the Liberation of Mozambique (FRELIMO) was established; the event was followed by the pursuit of political emancipation through military means that started in 1964. Mozambique eventually became an independent state in 1975. As the country began to enjoy the experience of freedom, another war broke out, shattering the dream of a prosperous future. This second war lasted for sixteen years before a peace agreement was eventually reached in 1992. Mozambique, like most postcolonial African nations, was negatively impacted by its colonial legacy. The country was subjected to several setbacks, such as political sieges, economic sabotage, and systemic attacks due to colonial inheritances after independence. The consolidation of the peace, democracy, and reconstruction processes has begun to bear fruit in Mozambique for the first time since 1964. The country now enjoys the longest period of stability in the following areas:

1. Multiparty elections that further consolidate its democratic process
2. The first succession of leadership between two living presidents since independence
3. An economic growth rate between 7 percent and 10 percent for ten years or more
4. The economic and social infrastructure devastated by war has gradually been rebuilt.
5. Investment in social sectors opened access to health and educational opportunities to millions of citizens
6. Confidence in the economy has been regained, and foreign investors are now returning in the country
7. The country's public finances are in reasonable shape, and development partners are supporting the country's commitment to reform.

As the country enters its fifteenth year of peace in 2015 following a brutal and destructive civil war, there are signs of continued democratic transformation, and pro-market economic reforms appear to be rosy. Mozambique continues to be placed on top of the list of the world's fastest-growing economies. This has been seen as another signal for Washington Consensus to provide the funds required to bring infrastructure, schools, and health care facilities to the rural majority. According to the United Nations Record, Mozambique is highlighted as one of the success stories in conflict-ridden Africa. Many in the international community have credit Mozambique's remarkable transformation to the UN's efforts to sustain the drawn-out peace negotiations and demobilize more than 90,000 soldiers, rebuild a unified national army, and foster the rise of a legitimate and peaceful opposition (Weistein, 2002). In response to Mozambique's role in the peace process, donor investments continue to support the country today, funding more than half of the government's annual budget.

In an article by Jeremy Weinstein, *"A Fading UN Success Story,"* the author described the UN's work in Mozambique as unprecedented in scope, with dramatic results. The UN's efforts have contributed to two conservative free elections and growth rates approaching 10 percent a year over the past decade and cannot be ignored. The presence of UNDP in building social capital in the country is another hopeful sign of the capacity for post-conflict development. UNDP assists countries like Mozambique that are coming out of brutal and destructive civil wars to build social capital. The UNDP's efforts also help to redesign institutional environments by building trust among the citizens and between citizens and the state. Building trust is a critical task in post-conflict reconstruction efforts. Preventing future conflict is not only a matter of keeping those with guns from using them but of establishing accountable, transparent, and participatory systems of authority (Fred-Mensah, 2004). The UNDP's good governance efforts also involve the development of a rule of law, transparency of public organizations, and the fostering of genuine popular participation in the political decision-making process, among other things.

However, there are some "bumps in the road" toward lasting peace and prosperity as Mozambicans from all walks of life learn to resolve problems through dialogue and democratic means. Examples of "bumps in the road" are issues such as the two bank failures, the assassination of the country's most respected independent journalist, and depreciation of the currency. There is evidence of fundamental divisions that threaten the future of Mozambique's democratic transition. In November 2000, police in the City of Montepuez killed a demonstrator who challenged the government, claiming to have won the national elections. The incident created tension that nearly exploded into large-scale violence. The fact remains that Mozambique, like many African countries, cannot deny the fact of its own challenges. Through the lens of those opposed to the government, Mozambique's political and economic situation may interpret the status of democracy in this post-conflict nation more bleakly.

THE ROLE OF CIVIL SOCIETY IN POST-CONFLICT LIBERIA

In January 2006, a democratically elected government emerged under the leadership of President Ellen Johnson Sirleaf. This period ushered in a new round in the peace-building process; civil society organizations saw themselves as key partners with the Liberian state. Since then, civil society groups have continued to demand space from the Liberian state. The involvement of civil organizations has also created a new level of expectations in state-civil relations in post-conflict Liberia. Until 2006, how the state and civil society organization coexisted or interacted in Liberia was not a major factor. Before the civil war, civil society organizations were not common or given real relevance. There were a few pressure groups, such as the trade unions, from private sectors that advocated for the interests of their members. However, much earlier in Liberia, as in most West African states, there were a number of civil society organizations, which were largely faith-based and involved in health, education, and agriculture.

These organizations primarily managed schools and hospitals throughout Liberia. As a result of their critical roles in society, their relationships with the state were cordial. It was not uncommon to find government officials present at the signing ceremonies for funding agreements and doing briefings on civil society organizations' activities (Atuobi, 2010). By the 1970s, the idea of a civil society movement had evolved in Liberia, when organizations such as the Movement for Justice in Africa (MOJA), a continental organization that seeks social justice, was attacking the status quo. Another CSO formed during the 1970s was the Progressive Alliance of Liberia. The objectives of the new groups at that time were primarily political. Their role in society included a push for radical changes or reforms and other demands on the state. Because the objectives of the civil society organizations before the civil war were demanding political reforms, accountability, and transparency, there was an antagonistic relationship between these groups and the state.

The period between 1989 and 1996 saw a rise of civil society organizations in Liberia. Some of the CSOs formed during this period include the Inter-Faith Mediation Committee (IFMC), the merging of the Liberia Council of Churches (LCC), and the National Muslim Council of Liberia

(NMCL). There were also a number of human rights organizations and women groups that played some critical roles during the Liberian civil conflict. Among these were the Catholic Justice and Peace Commission (CJC), the Center for Law and Human Rights Education (CLHRE), and the Liberian Women's Initiative (LWI). These groups, along with the Economic Community of West African States (ECOWAS) and the Cease-Fire Monitoring Group known as ECOMOG, played diverse roles to bring about resolution to the civil conflict in the country (Atuobi, 2010). When the Liberian civil conflict broke out again in 1999, civil society organizations resumed their involvement by searching for a peaceful resolution with participation in the peace talks in Accra, Ghana, in 2003.

With the outstanding roles of civil society organizations in Liberia after several decades now, one would think that this would have an impact on good governance. Liberia, like many African states, still struggles when it comes to instituting political reforms, transparency, and accountability. As a society, Liberians have a functionalist worldview; in other words, conducting business the same way and expecting different results. Theoretically, Liberia has a democracy as measured by election results, but that democracy is considered one of the hybrid regimes, according to an African Democracy rating in 2011. In other words, it has a partial democracy. It has had systemic problems for more than 150 years. In such a unitary state with strong centralized political power, radical social change can only come about through a selfless leader who is committed to real reforms across the board. As a head of the executive branch of government, that leader will have to be a transformative leader with an uncompromising national agenda. It will have to be someone capable of preaching the gospel of real reform to move the consciousness of his or her people. As Africa's oldest republic and a nation that is fashioned after the United States, it is morally imperative to be seen as an exemplary nation on the continent if these steps are taken.

THE ROLE OF YOUTH IN LIBERIA

African youth in Liberia and elsewhere on the continent no longer want to view themselves as future leaders of their society; instead they want to be viewed as leaders of today. They believe that they have ability to shape their own future. This twenty-first-century worldview has become engulfed across Africa due to the limited opportunities available to youth, driving them to become contributors to their communities. In the Liberian situation, it is critical because youth range from fifteen to thirty-five years old. The definition of youth is congruent with the constitution of Liberia and the International Convention on the Rights of the Child. With such an age differentiation, it is quite understandable why there is the need to become the leaders of today. Empowering youth in post-conflict Liberia is critical, because fifteen years of civil war impacted young Liberians in a negative way. During this period, youth were marginalized from the mainstream of the society or abused as child soldiers.

The civil war destroyed the lives of youth psychologically, socially, and economically, thereby setting the stage for peer pressure, prostitution, teenage pregnancy, and unemployment. Homelessness and unemployment have caused Liberian youth to roam the streets of Monrovia and other cities on a daily basis, having no place to go. It is estimated that over three thousand children roam the streets of Monrovia, many still lacking educational opportunities, health care, parental guidance, and other needed support (streetkidsnews.com). The contrary under normal circumstances would have given preparation as future leaders. In the post-conflict era, the youth have acknowledged their role in national development, demanding respect for their worldview. They are no longer willing to accept exclusion from participating in mainstream society. Youth make up 53 percent of the population of 5 million people, according to the recent national census. This means Liberia, like many developing nations, is largely populated by the young. Therefore, youth are important and have the potential to play a major role in decision making. As a result of this advocacy, a number of programs have been initiated to mitigate the issues.

SPECIFIC PROGRAMS FOR YOUTH DEVELOPMENT

In the national reconstruction plan for Liberia during the post-conflict era, several programs have been outlined for youth development. They include the Federation of Liberian Youth (FLY), created as an autonomous organization with the responsibility of organizing and coordinating activities for Liberian youth. The objectives include the strengthening of youth participation in policy implementation, promotion of youth rights, advocacy for inclusion in decision making, and ensuring youth commitment in the following areas:

- Information sharing
- Transparency
- Accountability
- Value-based leadership
- Decentralization of youth activities

The organization has created programs that engage youth collectively, as well as help them to develop practical leadership skills. It also enables youth from different tribes to work together as a team, a recipe for reconciliation in the post-conflict society.

The Ministry of Youth and Sports is another principle entity for youth-driven initiatives in Liberia. As part of the reconstruction plan, the agency implemented several projects in partnership with several international organizations, such as the United Nations and World Bank. The ministry, in partnership with USAID and World Bank–run Youth on the Job Training Program (YJTP) offers a nine-to-eighteen-month internship that places students with mentors who work in different sectors of the job market. Students who participate in the program choose their area of interest, ranging from carpentry to medicine, very similar to the Booker Washington Agricultural and Industrial High School in Kakata, about forty-two miles from Monrovia, the Liberian capital. At the end of the program, the students are certified and in some cases hired by the mentors.

The Ministry of Youth and Sports has also started a National Youth Volunteering Service Program (NYVSP). The program places high school and college students in different regions of the country to work for a period of time. Upon completion of the program, they are given a stipend. Apart from encouraging these young people to achieve something productive with their lives, it is a means for them to consider living elsewhere in the country. Technical and Vocation Education Training (TVET) was also created by the Ministry of Youth and Sports to increase the technical capacity of Liberian youth. The primary purpose of the training program is to increase human resources potential, an area that is at an all-time low in the country due to skilled workers leaving for better pay in developed countries. The majority of Liberian youth lived half of their lives during the conflict and have no former training to acquire skills necessary for the workforce. "It is a double-edge sword. Youth are not in school, but they have no skills to work. So, all is left is to engage in deviant behavior" (Woods, 2011). Some of these programs were created in previous governments but were discontinued due to the civil unrest in the country (Atuobi, 2010).

EXAMINING DEMOCRACY IN ZAMBIA

Overview

Political participation and democracy in Zambia provide a comprehensive review of the state of democracy and popular participation in government and public affairs (Roshnee, 2013). According to Open Society Initiative of Southern Africa's report, Zambia is one of the nations in southern Africa that has experienced unprecedented political development. Consequently, the country has held six general elections, including four peaceful presidential elections, since the return of multiparty politics and competitive elections for the parliament and presidency in October, 1991, when Zambia experienced a new movement known as the Movement for Multiparty Democracy (MMD). That movement replaced the one-party system that lasted from 1972 till 1991. The MMD came in with a commitment to consolidate a liberal democracy and a program of sweeping economic liberalization, allowing citizens to participate in local elections. Since then the country has initiated the making of the new constitution, a decision which was followed by the election of President Michael Sata and his Patriotic Front in 2011.

Michael Sata, a ferocious public speaker and career politician, grew close to President Frederick Chiluba, allowing him to serve several ministerial appointments during the Chiluba administration. In 2001, Sata broke away from the MMD and formed the Patriotic Front (PF). The PF gained support from the disillusioned population about the issue of underdevelopment and blatant corruption under the MMD. In 2011 the PF won the national elections, promising to put more money in the pockets of the people, a war against corruption, and a new people-driven constitution. The victory of President Sata was a welcome example of a peaceful transfer of power and the maturity of African democracy. The Zambian experience put the country in a position of continental leadership by keeping three campaign promises, revising the country's draft constitution to better protect basic freedom for its citizens, targeting corruption in the country, and protecting the rights of all Zambian workers, especially Zambians who are employed in a growing number of mining industries in the country owned and operated by the Chinese. According to a study on Zambia done the University of Warwick, the country is one of sixteen states in sub-Saharan Africa to have sustained democratic transition during the 1990s. The country's economy has grown at the healthy rate of 6.8 percent per annum since President Michael Sata took office.

Despite all the progress, challenges remain with some issues, such as constitutional and electoral rules, Zambia's democratic deficits, as experts have observed. The PF has been unable to implement some of the reforms it promised as the opposition party. Like most of Africa, a serious challenge in Zambia is tribalism. The long-standing fight to eradicate tribalism began during the presidency of Kenneth Kaunda, who also made the fight against tribalism his hidden mission with a message of "One Zambia, One Nation." During this same period, there were also reports of election flaws, causing the United Nations Independence Party to boycott the 1996 presidential and parliamentary elections. This report made Zambia the sixteen boycott in Africa that the study identified, along with twenty-seven further instances of election flaws coupled with allegations of fraud and other irregularities over the period between 1988 and 1999 (Burnell, 2001).

THE ZAMBIAN–CHINESE AGENDA

One of Africa's external challenges in the twenty-first century is managing the massive inflow of Chinese capital, a challenge that nearly every African country is faced with today. In Zambia, Chinese companies serve as vital financial resources to the Zambia economy. On the other hand, those resources bear the attitudes and standards that prevail in the Chinese labor market, according to a Freedom House report. Some of the challenges are the workplace safety and environmental impact that are often not given attention by Chinese investors. While it is true that Africa has a need for direct foreign investment, it is also critical that these enterprises comply with national labor laws and international standards. Zambia's democracy and reform efforts may be derailed if issues that affect its citizens' well-being are overlooked. Thomas Lansner (2015) asserts, "Investment agreements should also include other immunities such as skill and technology transfer and restrict the importation of Chinese workers if local labor force is available."

One of the challenges across Africa is the proliferation of small Chinese retail businesses (many of whom are working in these illegally) in many cities and towns, according to Freedom House report. These Chinese retail businesses often crowd out local enterprise and take their profits out of the country, because they have amazing commercial skills. One of the challenges during Michael Sata's administration is highlighting labor rights as key areas. These areas should be addressed to further promote democratic consolidation.

Some of the major decisions include ensuring that the new constitution requires presidential candidates to receive at least 50 percent of the popular vote to win an election, strengthening the court system, and reducing police misconduct (p. 3). Other reform efforts include empowering autonomous and genuine anticorruption initiatives in the government. These would not be possible without the vibrant and growing Zambian civil society, which has served as a source of advice and cooperation for the government without sacrificing its independent and critical watchdog role. Civil society has continued to remain a significant force behind reform and good governance, not just in Zambia but throughout Africa.

Zambia's success story of good governance and reform may have a caveat with the death of Michael Sata in 2014. Since that time, there has been a moment of disorder in Zambian politics (Hixon, 2015). The Zambia agenda is similar to that of most African leadership; whenever there is a change in leadership, the tendency exists for reluctance in promoting or carrying out programs from previous administrations or leadership, especially by opposition leaders. In the case of Zambia, former President

Rupiah Banda re-emerged, attempting to sidestep party leaders to never support Mumba. Interestingly, Mumba managed to secure the candidacy through a favorable court ruling without the support of the party. Rupiah Mumba did compete against nine other candidates who contested the election, with the two candidates who were considered the main contenders: Lungu and Hakainde Hichilema of the opposition party, the United Party for National Development (UPND). At the end of the day, Lungu emerged victorious, assuring the possibility for improvements to Zamia's democratic standing.

Lungu had a better advantage during the election because he had the support of those who believed that the Patriotic Front (PF) should finish President Michael Sata's term. Voters also remembered that after Sata's death, Lungu resisted the pressure to make a power grab by turning over the position of acting president to Vice President Guy Scot, as called for in the constitution. When President Lungu took over, he opened up a dialogue with the civil society and promised to solicit their input in the implementation of the NGO Act going forward. In Zambia, civil society comprised such entities as churches, businesses, professional associations, human rights groups, and other nongovernmental organizations committed to the creation of a democratic society. As acting president in the final days of President Sata's administration, Lungu was instrumental in releasing the long-awaited draft of the constitution. Lungu also went further to accommodate regulations that included civil society's input in the country, reforming the restrictive Public Order Act, and repairing relations with the media.

CONCLUSION

As you end this book, my hope is that you walk away with a better frame of mind about Africa and some of the issues that impact development, good governance, politics, and the roles of civil society and the international community. The hope is that you are walking away with an awareness about what's working in Africa that is not well known to the rest of the world or usually given little attention and credit. Creating this awareness, despite the challenges facing the continent, in potential readers is what this book is about. Synthesizing all the issues discussed in the book, you will walk away with an understanding of why this book was written. While it is impossible to address all the issues, this book has at least set the stage for more research, more dialogue, and more courage to understand what's working in Africa. It is my pleasure to escort you back in your world like you were before reading this book and makes the transition back to your daily lives but with a totally different worldview, as well as the knowledge and resources this book has provided, so you understand and are aware of what's working in Africa.

The analysis presented in this book should serve as conduit between readers and the people of Africa, especially readers interested in understanding the social dynamics and political developments currently taking place in Africa. The detailed account depicted in this book will serve as useful information in your desire to learn more about the transformation that has engulfed the continent. Throughout this book a number of issues were raised, issues such as the role of civil society and its relations with African states; regional cooperation in Africa; the process of democracy and good

151

governance, and how African nations are dealing with global challenges that face its people. Tremendous changes are taking place in Africa that are usually overlooked on the world stage. These "silent" developments have created assumptions that Africa cannot be taken seriously as a major player in the twenty-first century. My hope is that this book has served as a useful resource in providing an understanding about some of the misconceptions about Africa. When the decision to write this book was made about four years ago, my primary concerns were, what will it do for potential readers? Will it inform, educate, or provide solutions? Or will it challenge readers to start a new conversation about reform efforts in Africa? As you walk away from reading this book, you will be the judge in addressing these questions.

Whether foreign policy issues, democracy, or geopolitical concerns and the role of civil society, this book has made an attempt to address them. As Africa grapples with the challenges of the twenty-first century, it is critical to present to the world the right images and the significance of its contributions, not to place all the emphasis on challenges such as civil war, famine, mismanagement, corruption, and lack of good governance as the only order of the day. The title of the book, What's Working in Africa, was given to make a case that despite the challenges, progress is taking place across the continent, as indicated by a number of countries; the glass is still half full but on its way to becoming full. Reform and democracy are becoming success stories, not just regional phenomena but something that every region on the continent is experiencing.

My hope is that as you conclude your reading, I trust that the experience gained from reading this book will give you an opportunity to understand what is working in Africa. Ultimately, the author has made a case that will help you make the transition back into your daily lives again, this time walking away with a different worldview, one that will perhaps allow you to draw a different conclusion; hopefully this experience will enable you to appreciate the topics that were discussed in this book.

Acronyms and Abbreviations

1. ECOWAS = Economic Community of West African States
2. EAEC = East African Economic Community
3. NGO = Non-governmental Organization
4. UNITA = Universal Negro Improvement Association
5. DRC = Democratic Republic of Congo
6. OAU = Organization of African Unity
7. FAS = Federal African States
8. AU = African Union
9. EU = European Union
10. GDP = Gross Domestic Product
11. AGOA = African Growth and Opportunities Act
12. GSP = Generalized System of Preferences
13. MCA = Millennium Challenge Account
14. MCC = Millennium Challenge Corporation
15. UNESCO = United Nations Educational, Scientific and Cultural Organization
16. AFRICOM = African Commend
17. CBO = Community-based Organization
18. WDR = World Development Report
19. MRU = Mano River Union
20. SADC = Southern African Development Community
21. FOSDA = Foundation for Security and Development in Africa
22. ONUB = United nations organization in Burundi

23. MUNOC = United Nations Organization Mission in the Democratic Republic of Congo
24. NMOG = National Military Observer Group
25. USSR = Union of Soviet Socialist Republic
26. IMF = International Monetary Fund
27. SCPR = Civil Society for Poverty Reduction
28. HIPC = Heavily Indebted Poor Countries
29. CSCQBE = Civil Society Coalition for Quality Basic Education
30. CBA = Center for Budget Advocacy
31. MEJN = Malawi Economic Justice Network
32. UNDP = United Nations Development Program
33. PBB = Program-Based Budgeting
34. CABRI = Collective African Budget Institute
35. GNI = Gross National Income
36. IPP = Investment Project Planning
37. ESTP = Economic and Social Transformation Plan
38. LMS = Learning Management System
39. PFM = Public Finance Management
40. IPAC = Inter-Party Advisory Committee
41. APIGC = African Party for the Independence of Guinea-Bissau and Cape Verde
42. EBRD = European Bank for reconstruction and Development
43. TANU = Tanganyika African National Union
44. USAID = United States Agency for International Development
45. SADCC = Southern African Development Coordination Conference
46. ANC = African National Congress
47. PAC = Pan African Congress
48. ZANU = Zimbabwe African National Union
49. TRC = Truth and Reconciliation Commission
50. PLO = Palestine Liberation Organization
51. ENTC = Ethiopian National Transition Council
52. ADB = African Development Bank
53. GPP = Governance and Peace Program
54. PACE = Parliamentarian Assistance and Civil Engagement
55. NEEDS = National Economic Empowerment Development Strategy

56. SEEDS = State Economic Empowerment Development Strategy
57. NMG = National Millennium Goal
58. GBS = General Budgeting Support
59. ANEC = Autonomous National Election Commission
60. SWAPO = South West Africa People's Organization
61. PLAN = People's Liberation Army of Namibia
62. WCG = Western Contact Group
63. VOA = Voice of America
64. EAC = East African Community
65. IFMC = Inter-Faith Mediation Committee
66. LCC = Liberia Council of Churches
67. NMCL = National Muslim Council of Liberia
68. CJPC = Catholic Justice and Peace Commission
69. CLHRE = Center for Law and Human Rights Education
70. LWI = Liberian Women Initiative
71. FLY = Federation of Liberian Youth
72. YJTP = Youth on the Job Training Program
73. NYVSP = National Youth Volunteering Service Program
74. TVET = Technical and Vocational Education Training
75. MMD = Movement for Multiparty Democracy
76. PF = Patriotic Front
77. UPND = United Party for National Development

GLOSSARY

1. **Colonialism** = the control or governing influence of a nation over a dependent country, territory, or people.
2. **Accountability** = the quality or state of being accountable; especially: an obligation or willingness to accept responsibility or to account for one's action.
3. **Strategic planning** = A systemic process of envisioning a desired future, and translating this vision into broadly defined goals or objectives and a sequence of steps to achieve them.
4. **Demilitarization** = deprive of military use character; free from militarism; or to place under civil instead of military control.
5. **Decentralization** = the dispersion or distributions of function and power from central authority to regional and local authority.
6. **Sustainability** = the ability to be sustained, supported, upheld, or confirmed.
7. **Articulate** = uttered clearly in distinct syllables; expressed, formulated, or presented with clarity and effectiveness.
8. **Socialism** = any of various economic and political theories advocating collective or governmental ownership and administration of the means of production and distribution of goods.
9. **Capitalism** = an economic system in which investment ownership of the means of production, distribution, and exchange of wealth is made and maintained chiefly by private individuals or corporations; contrary to state-owned means of wealth.

10. **Protectorate** = a relationship of protection and partial control assumed by a superior power over a dependent country or region.

11. **Exemplary** = Serving as an example, instance or illustration.

12. **Post-colonialism** = the study of the legacy of the era of European, and sometimes American, direct global domination, which ended roughly in the mid-20th century, and the residual political, socio-economic, and psychological effects of the colonial history.

13. **Exemplar** = a person or thing serving as a typical example or appropriate model.

14. **Geopolitical** = a combination of political and geographic factors relating to something (as a state or particular resources; a governmental policies guided by geopolitics; or the study of geographic factors and their influences on power relationships in international politics.

15. **Intensity** = the quality or state of being intense; extreme degree of strength, force, energy or feeling.

16. **Emancipate** = to free from restrain, control, or power of another; especially from free from bondage.

17. **Colonial** = of, relating to, or characteristic of a colony.

18. **Idealism** = the practice of forming ideals or living under their influence; something that is **idealized.**

19. **Romanticism** = a movement in the arts and literature that originated in the late 18th century, emphasizing inspiration, subjectivity, and the primacy of the individual.

20. **Gradualist** = the belief in or the policy of advancing toward a goal by gradual, often slow stages.

21. **Functionalist** = a person who advocates, or works according to, the principles of functionalism.

22. **Integration** = the act or instance of combining into an integral whole; an act or instance of integrating or combining racial, religious, or ethnic group.

23. **Sovereignty** = supreme power especially over a body politic; freedom from external control: Autonomy

24. **Constitutive** = having the power to enact or establish: constitutive; relating to, or dependent on constitution.

25. **Transatlantic slavery** = the business or process of procuring, transporting, and selling slave; especially black Africans to the New world prior to the 19ᵗʰ century.
26. **Imperialism** = the policy, practice, or advocacy of extending the power and dominion of a nation especially by direct territorial acquisitions or by gaining indirect control over the political and economic life of other areas.
27. **Neocolonialism** = the policy of indirectly exerting political and cultural influence over another country or entity; especially a formal colony.
28. **Predicament** = an unpleasant difficult, perplexing or dangerous situation.
29. **Multifaceted** = having many facets or aspects or having many aspects phases.
30. **Extraordinary** = beyond what is usual, ordinary, or established; exceptional in character, amount, degree, etc.
31. **Globalization** = the act or process of globalizing; or the state of being globalized.
32. **Socioeconomic** = of, relating to, or involving a combination of social and economic factors.
33. **Demographics** = a single vital or social statistics of a human population, as the number of births or deaths; a specific segment of a population having shared characteristics.
34. **Methodology** = a body of methods, rules, and postulates employed by a discipline: a particular procedure or set of procedures.
35. **Sensationalized** = to present in a sensationalized manner.
36. **Sensitivity** = the quality or state of being sensitive; the capacity of being easily hurt.
37. **Exploitation** = use or utilization, especially for profit; the act of employing to the greatest possible advantage; the use or manipulation of another person for one's own advantage.
38. **Monopoly** = exclusive ownership through legal privilege, command of supply, or concert action; exclusive possession or control.
39. **Unilaterally** = done or undertaken by one person or party; of, relating to, or affecting one side of a subject.

40. **Nonintervention** = abstention by a nation from interference in the affairs of other nations or in those of its own political subdivision; failure or refusal to intervene.

41. **Multilateralism** = involving more than two nations or parties or the practice of promoting trade among several countries through agreement concerning quantity and price of commodities, as the common market, and sometime restricted tariffon goods from outside.

42. **Marshall Plan** = a program by which the United States gave over 12 billion of economic aid to Western Europe to help them rebuild after the devastation of World War II.

43. **Conspicuously** = easily seen or noticeable; readily visible or observable or attracting special attention, as by outstanding qualities.

44. **Instrumental** = serving or acting as an instrument or means; useful; helpful.

45. **Devastated** = destroy, sack, ruin or level.

46. **Bureaucracy** = a body of non-elective government officials; an administrative policy-making group.

47. **Paradigms** = a standard, perspective, or set of ideas; a way of looking at things.

48. **Post-conflict** = reconstruction aims at the consolidation of peace and security and the attainment of sustainable socio-economic development in a war-shattered country.

49. **Mitigate** = a lessening the force or intensity of something unpleasant, as wrath, pain, grief, or extreme circumstances.

50. **Ammunitions** = the material fired, scattered, dropped, or detonated from any weapon, as bombs or rockets, and especially shot, shrapnel, bullets, or shells fired by gun.

51. **Proliferation** = to grow or produce by multiplication of parts, as in budding or cell division, or procreation.

52. **Humanitarian** = a person actively engaging in promoting human welfare and social reforms, as a philanthropist.

53. **Marginalized Group** = to be confined to lesser or lower social standing; the social process of becoming or being made marginalized (especially as a group within the larger society); the marginalization of the underclass.

54. **Strategies** = a careful plan or method; a choice of going about doing things.

55. **Social accountability** = the measure that are made by organization to be aware of concerns to the community surrounding it; a commitment to the health and safety, civil and human rights and betterment of the community.

56. **Upward accountability** = is when organization is accountable up to organizational chain to owner, the board or donors.

57. **Downward accountability** = is when the organization is accountable to the people they aim to help, such as the beneficiaries.

58. **Accentuate** = to emphasize a particular feature of something or to make something more noticeable.

59. **Genocide** = the murder of a whole group of people, especially a whole nation, race, or religion.

60. **Noninterference** = the policy or practice of refraining from interference, especially in political affairs.

61. **Complexity** = the quality or state of not being simple; a part of something that is not complicated or hard to understand.

62. **Preservation** = to keep alive or in existence; to preserve liberties as free citizens.

63. **Reconstruction** = the act or process of rebuilding something, or a recreation of past events, the period after the Civil War in southern United States.

64. **Inextricably** = of, relating to, or being the period of time before colonization of a region or territory.

65. **Pre-colonial** = of or relating to the time before a region or country became a colony.

66. **Pre-modern** = the period in society which came prior to modernity or modern era.

67. **Assassination** = to kill suddenly or secretively, especially a political prominent person.

68. **Paramilitary** = noting or pertaining to an organization operating as, in place, or as a supplement to a regular military force; a paramilitary police unit.

69. **Duplicitous** = the act of being sneaky or deceitful; an example of duplicitous is someone who always lies to get his or her way.

70. **Expatriate** = a person who lives outside of their native country; or a person who has citizenship in at least one country, but who is living in another country.

71. **Secessionist** = the withdrawal of a group from a large entity, especially a political entity.

72. **Unilaterally** = of, on, relating to, involving, or affecting only one side; performing or undertaken by one side.

73. **Ombudsman** = a government officials (as in Sweden or New Zealand) appointed to received and investigated complaints made by individuals against abuses or capricious acts of public officials.

74. **Opportunistic** = to be opportunistic is to quickly take advantage of a situation, usually in a way that is just plain wrong.

75. **Perpetrator** = a perpetrator is someone who has committed a crime or at least done something bad.

76. **Disillusionment** = disappointment that you feel when you realize something you thought was true was not.

77. **Disseminate** = to scatter or spread widely, as though sowing seed; to broadcast; disperse; or promulgate extensively.

78. **Participatory** = to take or have a part or share, as with others; or partake; or participate in a play.

79. **Proliferation** = to grow or multiply by rapidly producing new tissue, parts, cells, or offspring; to increase or spread at a rapid rate.

80. **Refinement** = the act or process of improving something or bringing something to a pure state; as refinement of sugar.

81. **Extractive** = of, relating to, or involving extraction; tending toward or resulting in withdrawal of natural resources by extraction with no provision for replenishment.

82. **Millennium** = a millennium is a period of one thousand years.

83. **Cumbersome** = hard to handle or manage because of size or weight, as in cumbersome in a sentence.

84. **Hybrid regimes** = found in most developing countries, especially since the end of Cold War. They are called Hybrid Regimes they combined democratic traits (e.g. frequent and direct election) with autocratic ones (e.g. political repression).

85. **Predicated** = to base or establish (a statement or action, for example), I predicated my argument on the facts.

86. **Parliamentary** = the highest legislative authority in Britain, consisting of the House of Commons, which exercises effective power, the House of Lords, and the sovereign.

87. **Despotically** = meaning, what is despot: a person, especially a ruler, who has unlimitedauthority; a person who wields power oppressively; a tyrant.

88. **Self-determination** = free choice of one's own acts or state without external compulsion.

89. **Universal suffrage** = the extension of voting rights to all citizens without restriction based on race, sex, religious belief, wealth or social status.

90. **Sophisticated** = having a good understanding of the way people behave and/or a good knowledge of culture; having a refined knowledge of the ways of the world cultivated especially through wide experience.

91. **Complacent** = a feeling of being satisfied with how things are and not wanting to try to make them better; a complacent feeling or condition.

92. **Rehabilitation** = to restore to a former capacity: reinstate; to restore to good repute.

93. **Predominant** = having ascendency, power, authority, or influence over others or preeminent.

94. **Autonomy** = the state of existing or acting separate from others; self-government or the right of self-government.

95. **Universal adult franchise** = this means all citizens who's age is above18 have the right to vote; in other words, all citizens except lunatics, minors or aliens.**Electorate** = the body of persons entitled to vote in an election; a body of qualified voters.

96. **Infrastructure** = the basic physical and organizational structures and facilities; (as in buildings, roads, power supplies) needed for the operation of a society or enterprise: the social and economic infrastructure of a country.

97. **Accessibility** = easy to approach, reach, enter, speak with or use.

98. **Retrenchment** = forced lay-off of employees by a firm, usually to cut down its payroll.

99. **Cumulative** = increasing or enlarging by successive addition.
100. **Nepotism** = favoritism (as in appointment to job) bases on kinship.
101. **Sectionalism** = excessive or narrow-minded concern for local or regional interests as opposed to the interest of a whole.
102. **Tribalism** = a strong feeling of identity with and loyalty to one's tribe or group; a very strong feeling of loyalty to your tribe.
103. **Negligible** = so small, unimportant, etc, as to be not worth considering; insignificant.
104. **Repercussion** = an often indirect effect, influence, or result that is produced by an event or action.
105. **Differentiation** = to form or mark differently from such things; distinguish; to identify the differences between things, to discriminate among them.
106. **Parliament** = a representative body having supreme legislative powers within a state or multinational organization.
107. **Patronage** = the support, encouragement, privilege, or financial aid that an organization or individual bestows to another.
108. **Incumbent** = one that occupies a particular position or place.
109. **Stagnation** = the state of being still, or not moving, like a sitting puddle of water where stagnation attracts mosquitoes.
110. **Perfunctory** = meaning, what is perfunctory: done quickly, without taking care or interest.
111. **Marginalization** = to place in a position of marginal importance, influence, or power; to relegate or confine to a lower or outer limit or edge, as of social standing.
112. **Concession** = the act of yielding or conceding, as to a demand or argument; something that is allowed or given up, often in order to end a disagreement.
113. **Post-protectorate** = a state or country that protected by a larger, stronger one; state was protected by a larger one.
114. **Coincidental** = existing or occurring or the same time.
115. **Coup d'état** = a sudden attempt by a small group of people to take over the government usually through violence.
116. **Transformation** = a thorough or dramatic change in form or appearance; to change in form, appearance, or structure; metamorphose.

117. **Conciliation** = to bring two opposing sides together to reach a compromise in an attempt to avoid taking a case to a trail.
118. **Mata-analysis** = the statistical procedure for combining data from multiple studies.
119. **Anti-colonial** = a person or country that actively opposes colonialism.
120. **Upheaval** = a great change, especially causing or involving much difficulty, actively, or trouble.
121. **Repatriation** = to bring or send back (a person, especially a prisoner of war, a refugee, etc) to his or her country or land of citizenship.
122. **Monopoly** = exclusive control by one group of the means of producing or selling a commodity or service.
123. **Privatization** = the process of transferring an enterprise or industry from the public sector to the private sector.
124. **Transparency** = the characteristic of being easy to see through; the quality of being easily seen through.
125. **Bellwether** = one that serves as a leader or as a leading indicator of future trends; someone or something that shows how a situation will develop of change.
126. **Unimaginable** = something that is unimaginable is difficult to imagine because it is so bad, good, big, etc.
127. **Post-revolutionary** = post revolution is the period right after the revolution.
128. **Socioeconomic** = of, relating to, or involving a combination of social and economic factors; related to the differences between groups of people caused mainly by their financial status.
129. **Tanganyika** = a formal country of east-central Africa; awarded to Britain in the breakup of German East Africa after World War 1, Tanganyika became independent in 1961.
130. **Rude awaking** = a sudden and often unwelcome realization: example "they all think Mr. McCrea has plenty of money, but they're due for a due for rude awakening.
131. **Socialism** = an economic and political system based on public or collective ownership of the means of production.
132. **Capitalism** = an economic system in which investment in and ownership of the means of production, distribution, and exchange

of wealth is made and maintained chiefly by private individual s or corporations, especially as contrasted to cooperatively or state- means of wealth.

133. **Consolidation** = the merger of two or more commercial interests or corporations.

134. **Retribution** = something done to get back at someone or the act of punishing someone for their actions.

135. **Dispensation** = an exemption or release from an obligation or rule, granted by or as if by an authority.

136. **Charismatic** = of, having, or characteristic of charisma; that which reduces to a mixture of charm and status.

137. **Hegemony** = leadership or predominant influence exercised by one nation over others, as in a confederation.

138. **Apartheid** = a racist political policy in South Africa demanding segregation of the nation's white and non-white populations.

139. **Servitude** = a condition in which one lacks liberty to determine one's course of action or way of life.

140. **Autonomous** = having the right or power of self-government; undertaken or carried on without outside control.

141. **Subjugation** = to bring under complete control or subjection; conquer; master or to bring under control, especially by military force; conquer.

142. **Philanthropic** = the effort or inclination to increase the well-being of humankind, as by charitable aid or donations; love of humankind in general.

143. **Africaners** = Africaners are Southern African ethnic group descended from predominantly Dutch settlers first arriving in the seventeenth and eighteenth centuries.

144. **Imperial** = of, relating to, befitting, or suggestive of an empire or an emperor.

145. **Insurgency** = as an organized resistance movement that uses subversion, sabotage, and armed conflict to achieve...

146. **Deterioration** = to make or become worse or inferior in character, quality, value, etc; to disintegrate or wear away.

147. **Orchestrate** = to compose or arrange (as in music) for performance by an orchestra; to arrange or control the elements of.

148. **Indispensable** = something or someone that is so good or important that you could not neglect or disregard.
149. **Unitary** = of, or relating to a system of government in which executive, legislative and judicial powers of each state in a body are vested in a central authority.
150. **Fugitive** = a person who flees or tries to escape; especially: refugee; something elusive or hard to find.
151. **Immobility** = is the state of not being able to move around or incapable of moving or being moved.
152. **Mau Mau Movement** = the **Mau Mau** Uprising, also the **Mau Mau** Revolt, or Kenya Emergency, was a military conflict that took place in British Kenya between 1952 1ⁿᵈ 1960.
153. **Commonwealth** = a group of sovereign states and their dependencies associated by their own choice and linked with common; the people of a nation or state; the body politic.
154. **Nutritional** = the process of taking in food and using it for growth, metabolism, and repair or the act or process of nourishing or nourished.
155. **Disproportionate** = out of proportion, as in size, shape, or amount; having or showing a difference that is not fair, reasonable, or expected.
156. **Detrimental** = causing damage or harm; injurious; or harmful or tending to cause harm.
157. **Multidimensional** = having or involving or marked by several dimensions or aspects.
158. **Deprivation** = to keep something away from someone; or a removal of rank or office.
159. **Attitudinal** = relating to one's feeling, mood or manner of acting; or a manner of thinking, feeling, or behavior that reflects a state of mind or disposition.
160. **Harmonizing** = to bring or come into agreement or harmony.
161. **Degenerate** = a person who has declined, as in morals or character, from a type or standard consider; having declined, as in function or nature or from a former or original state.
162. **Consortium** = a group made of two or more individuals, institutions, companies or governments, that work together toward achieve a chosen objective.

163. **Indignation** = strong displeasure at something considered unjust, offensive, insulting, or base; righteous anger.

164. **Escalate** = to increase in extend, volume, number, amount intensity, or scope; as to escalate a war.

165. **Constitutionalism** = advocacy of a system of government according to constitutional principles; or government in which power is distributed and limited and limited by a system of laws that must be obeyed by the ruler.

166. **Manifestation** = the act of disclosing what is secret, unseen or obscure; or public display of emotion or feeling, or something theoretical made real.

167. **Fragmentation** = the scattering of the fragments of an exploding bomb or other projectile; the act or process of breaking into fragments.

168. **In cohesive** = lacking integration; or the act or state of cohering, uniting, or sticking together.

169. **Macroeconomic** = the study of the large economic systems of s country or region; or the branch of economics dealing with the broad and general aspects of an economy.

170. **Deregulation** = the act of removing government legislation and laws in a particular market; to remove government regulatory controls from an industry, a commodity, etc.

171. **Liberalization** = is a relaxation of government restrictions, usually in such areas of social, political and economic policy.

172. **Privatization** = to transfer from public or government control or ownership to private enterprise.

173. **Impediment** = anything that slows or blocks progress such as how piracy is an impediment or obstacle to the pleasure cruise industry in Somalia.

174. **Ancestry** = a person's ethnic origin or descent, roots, or heritage, or the place; or the line of descent: lineage.

175. **Perspective** = a particular way of considering something; or the way that one looks at something.

176. **Exemplary** = deserving imitation because of excellence; or an excellent model or an example, or a sample, or worthy person or thing.

177. **Incumbent** = the person who is already in an elected office. An example of incumbent is the person who is currently the president.
178. **Remittances** = an amount of money that is sent as a payment for something.
179. **Communes** = a group of people living together in a shared community; or an intentional community of people living together, sharing common interests, etc.
180. **Mandate** = a formal order from a superior court or official to an inferior one; or an official command or a go-ahead.
181. **Infiltrate** = to pass through gaps, particularly into enemy lines or in the case of liquid passing through a substance.
182. **Transnational** = extending or going beyond national boundaries or extending or operating across national boundaries.
183. **Multilateral** = is multiple countries working in concert on a given issue or involving more than two nations or parties.
184. **Manipulation** = to control or play upon by artful, unfair, insidious means especially to one's advantage.
185. **Municipal** = of or relating the government of a city or town; of or relating to a town or city or its local government: municipal elections.
186. **Profitability** = the state or condition of yielding a financial profit or gain: it is often measured by price to earnings ratio.
187. **Levity** = a silly or light speech or behavior, usually at an inappropriate time. An example of levity is someone is being disrespectful to police.
188. **Revitalization** = to make (someone or something) active, healthy, or energetic again; or impact new life or vigor to something.
189. **Eradication** = to remove or destroy; or to remove (something) completely.
190. **Voyage** = a course of travel or passage, especially a long journey by water to a distance place.
191. **Trajectory** = a path, progression, or line of development resembling a physical trajectory: (as an upward career trajectory).
192. **Sabotage** = destructive or obstructive action carried on by a civilian or enemy agent to hinder a nation's war effort.

193. **Emancipate** = to free from bondage, oppression, or restraint; liberate.
194. **Demobilize** = to release (someone or something) from military service; or discharge (a person) from military service.
195. **Assassination** = to murder (usually a prominent person) by sudden or secrete attack often for political reasons.
196. **Antagonistic** = actively opposing or showing unfriendliness towards something or someone.
197. **Hybrid** = a mixture of two different things, resulting in somethings that has a little bit of both; (as in autocratic or democratic political systems).
198. **Consciousness** = the state of being conscious; awareness of one's own existence, sensations, thoughts, surroundings, etc.
199. **Engulf** = to flow over and enclose: overwhelm; (as the mounting seas threatened to engulf the island).
200. **Ferocious** = characterized by or showing extreme aggressiveness or violence; or frightening and violent.
201. **Disillusion** = to make someone realize their belief isn't true; or to cause to lose naïve faith and trust.
202. **Comprehensive** = complete and including everything that is necessary; or covering completely or broadly: inclusive; (as comprehensive examinations).
203. **Immunities** = protection or exemption from something, especially an obligation or penalty; or exempt from service or obligation.
204. **Misconception** = a mistaken thought, idea, or notion; a misunderstanding; or mistaken notion
205. **Phenomena** = something that is remarkable or extraordinary; a remarkable or exceptional person; prodigy.

BIBLIOGRAPHY

Marit Woods, (2011) A National Youth Policy, *Policy for Liberia: A Framework for Setting*

Adamolekum, L, *Commitment to Civil Service Reform in Africa (*unpublished paper, 2005*).*

African Studies Quarterly, Volume 14, Issues 1 & 2 (November 2013). http://www.africa.ufl.edu/asq/pdfs/v14i1-2a6.pdf

Atuobi, S. *State-Civil Society's Interface in Liberia's Post-Conflict Rebuilding Kaipt* (2010. *Occasional Paper, no. 30.*

Badger, S. and Cafiero, G. (2014) *Burkina Faso's West African Spring* (Africa,

Democracy, and Human Rights), *A joint publication of TheNation.com and Foreign Policy IN Focus*

Baker, B. "Seychelles: Democratizing in the Shadows of the Past." *Journal of Contemporary African Studies* (2008).

Bujra, A. (2002). *What Role for Civil Society and Other Stakeholders? Development Policy Management Forum (DPMF): Report of the Conference on the Challenges of Globalization to Democratic Governance in Africa*, p. 11–15.

Burnell, P. "The First Two Movements for Multiparty Democracy Administration in Zambia: Millennium Dawn or Millennium Sunset?" *Contemporary Politics* 7, no. 2 (2001).

Burnell, P. "Legislative-Executive Relations in Zambia: Parliamentary Reform on the Agenda." *Journal of Contemporary Studies* (2003).

Crain, J. and Stivachtis, Y. *Journal of Political and Military Sociology*37, no 2 (2009): 229–243.

Dandashly, A. The Holy Trinity of Democracy, Economic Development, and Security, EU Democratization Efforts beyond its Borders–The Case of Tunisia (2012).

Darga, L. A. (1998). *Social Dynamics and the Competitive Model of a Multiparty System: Case Study of Mauritius in Democracy and the One-Party State in Africa*, p.3-10.

DeLue, S. *Political Thinking, Political Theory, and Civil Society*. Longman, NY: 2002.

EISA report: *Electoral Institute for Sustainable Democracy in Africa* (2005).

Ezeh, P. "Buhari's Nigeria: Now, the Bigger Task," *New African Report* (2015).

Fadakinte, M. M. *"The Nature and Character of the Nigerian State: Explaining Election Crisis in a Peripheral State." British Journal of Arts and Social Sciences* 12, no. 11 (2013): 275–287. Fadakinte, M. M. (2002). *The Nigerian State and Transition Politics, in Browue Onuoha and M. M. Fadakinte (ed) Transition Politics in Nigeria, 1970–1999, Malthouse Press, Lagos.*

Fiori, A. *African and Asian Studies* 9. Issue ½ (2010): p. 83–101.

Ford, N. "Two-Speed Rwanda Attracts Investment," *New African* (2010). No. 501.

Fred-Mensah, B. K. *Social Capital Building as Capacity for Post-conflict Development: The UNDP in Mozambique and Rwanda. Global Governance: A Review of Multilateralism and International Organizations*10, no. 4, (2004): 437–457.

Gilbert, C. and Mureriwa, J. *Freedom House on Governance and Democracy in Southern Africa.* (2014).

Gordon, D. R. (). *Deepening democracy through community dispute resolution: problems and prospects in South Africa and Chile: Contemporary Justice Review.* Vol. 14 Issue 3 (2011): 291–305. 15p. DOI: 10.1080/10282580.2011.589667.

Guha, K. "Back in Business (Sierra Leone's President and CEO)," *Harvard International Review* (2009).

Guseh, J.S. and Oritsejafor, E. *Journal of Third World Studies*22, no.2 (2005): 121–137.

Guy, M. *Dream of Unity: From the United States of Africa to the Federation of African States.* Winston-Salem State University: 2011.

Habib, A. (2005) State-Civil Society Relation in Post-Apartheid South Africa Civil Society; Race Relations; Apartheid; Mass Society; Intergroup Relations; Twentieth Century. *South Africa 72, no. 3:*671–692.

Halperin, M, Single, J. and Weinstein, M. (2010) *How Democracies Promote Prosperity and Peace. (New York, NY: Rev. edn)*

Hixon, K. "Election Represents an Opportunity for Reform in Zambia," Freedom House Report, 2015.

Hornsby, C. *Kenya: A History Since Independence.* London: I. B. Tauris (2012):1 84885 886 2, 958.

Kaba, A. J. "Africa's Development in the Era of Barack Obama." *The Journal of Pan African Studies 2,* no.9 (2009).

Kabukuru, W. *Seychelles: A parable of success. Victoria, NewAfrican Magazine* (2014).

Kargbo, J. A. *The Sierra Leone Experience.* (2000).

Kellay, A. *One year of Koroma: The New African Report.* (2008).

Lansner, T. R. "After a Democratic Power Transfer, Zambia Must Tackle Chinese Investment Issues and Human Rights Reforms," Freedom House Report (2011).

Lindeke, W. A. *Human Rights and Democratic Transitions in Namibia: Critical New Perspectives* (1996).

Lobban, R. *Democracy and Elections in Cape Verde and Guinea-Bissau (African Studies and Anthropology, Rhode Island College* (1996).

Mallya, E. (2015) *A Critical Look at Tanzania's Development Vision 2025;* "Tanzania / Human Development Reports" Hdr.undp.org. N.P., 2015.Web.2015

Martin, P., Martin, S., and Weil, P. "Best practice Options: Mali." *International Migration*1, 40 (3) (2002).

McGreal, C. (2013) *Nelson Mandela: How Africa has changed in his lifetime.* www.the guardian.com (2013) the United Kingdom.

Meyns, P. "Cape Verde: An African Exception." *Journal of Democracy* (2002).

Moestrup, S. Benin—Democracy Battered. 2014

Murithi, T. *African Union: Pan-Africanism, Peacebuilding, and Development.* 2005.

Ngomane, T. and Flanagan, C. "The Road to Democracy in South Africa." *Peace Review*15, no. 3(2003): 267.

Nyerere, J. K. *Freedom and Socialism/ Uhuru naUmoja, A Selection from Writings and Speeches, 1965–1967, Dar-es-Salaam,* Oxford University Press.1976.

Nyirabu, M. "The Multiparty Reform Process in Tanzania: The Dominance of the Ruling Party." *African journal of political science; Vol.* 7, no. 2 (2002).

O'Keefe, M. T. "Of Seychelles and Seychelles." *The Saturday Evening Post* (2012)

Ongaro, W. A. *Good Governance: Key to Socio-economic development and poverty reduction.* (2006).

Phiri, I. *The Role of Civil Society in Press Freedom* (2015).

Priorities and Executing Action. Monrovia, Liberia

Ronning, H. *Election Processes, Liberation Movements and Democratic Change in Africa:* Department of Media and Communication, University of Oslo (2010).

Schneider, J. (2015) "Buhari's foreign policy closer to home than America." *New African Magazine Report; London*

Sckroter, E. "The African Governance Crisis." *Public Policy Analysis* (2010): 1–12.

Seyoum, B. "Export performance of developing countries under the Africa Growth and Opportunity Act." *Journal of Economic Studies*34, no. 6 *(2007):*

Singh, A. *"Renewable energy in the Pacific Island Countries-resources, politics and issues",* Mgmt of Env. Quality, 23(3) pp. 254-263*The University of the South Pacific.* (2012). www.usp.ac.fj....Staff Information

Singh, L. M. *Election and Democracy: Lessons to Be Learnt from Mauritius* www.academia.edu/.../Election and _Democracy _Lessons (2012), 1–15.

Siollun, M. "Iron Man: Buhari's Last Chance." https://www.questia.com/magazine/1G1...iron-man-buhari-s-last-chance *The New African Report* (2015).

Sromberg, D. *Media Development and Political Stability-* www.mediamapresource.org/ *The media Map* (2004)

Suntoo, R.) "The Need for Good Governance in Multi-Ethnic Societies." *World Journal of Social Sciences* 2. no.7 (2012) 4–6.

Throup, D. W. & Hornsby, C. *Multiparty Politics in Kenya: The Kenyatta and Moi States and the Triumph of the System in the 1992 Election.* (2005).

Tucker, V. *Divergence and Decline: The Middle East and the World after the Arab Spring.* (2012).

Weinstein, J. M. "Mozambique: A Fading UN Success Story." *Journal of Democracy, 13.1,* (2002):141–156.

Woods, M. *The Role of Youth in Post-Conflict Reconstruction: The Case Study of Liberia* (2011).

Yusuf, B. and Hedberg, C. J. *Democracy and Social Policy Development: Introduction and Overview of Democratization and Social Policy Development.* (2007).

Martin, G. (2013). *Dream of Unity: From the United Sates of Africa to the Federation of African States. African and Asian studies,* Vol. 12 issue 3.

Rotberg, R. (2007). *Improving nation – state governance.* Vol. 136, issue 1.

Rotberg, R. (2008). *Governance and Leadership in Africa: measures, methods, and results. Journal of International Affairs.*

Merill, 2006; Williams, (2005):*South Africa's ten years of democracy: development and media discourse. Vol. 23, issue 3.*

Patricia, D. (2012). *Conflict resolution in the great lakes region of Africa. Third world quarterly journal.*

Lindeke, W.A. (1995). *Democratization in Namibia: Soft state, hard choices. Studies in comparative international development.* Vol. 30, no. 1.

Backlander, C. (2013). *A look at Ethiopia after MelesZenawi.* Swedish magazine report.

Fadakinte, M. (1999-2012). *Civil society, democracy and good governance in Nigeria.* International journal of modern social sciences.

Gurirab, T.B. (2010).*Women in politics: the fight to end violence against women;* UN Chronicle vol. 47, issue 1.

Mallya, E. (2014). *A criticallook at Tanzania's Development vision 2025* Unpan1.un.org/intradoc/groups/public.documents.

Sengo, A. (2014). *Training for legal aid group provides information on human rights legislation;* USAID country report.www.usaid.gov/tanzania

Walker, C. & Tucker, V. (2011). *Tunisia: Arab Spring's pivotal democratic example. The Freedom House policy brief report.*

Kaba, A. J. (2007). *Africa's development in the era of Barack Obama: the role of the African Union.* Journal of Pan-African Studies vol. 7.

Commander, M. (2007). *Ghana at fifty: Moving towards Kwame Nkrumah's Pan-African Dream.* American quarterly vol. 59, issue 2.

McDougal, S. (2009). *African Foreign Policy: A question of methodology;* Journal of Pan African Studies. Vol. 2, issue 2.

Ehresman, T. (2012). *Foreign Direct Investment through the lens of the dhry, (1993)* studies association.

Payne, D. (2012). *African Democracy: NewYork Amsterdam News;* vol. 103, issue 10.

National Assessment Report, (2010). *SIDS Action through the implementation of Mauritius' strategy for implementation (MSI)*

UNDP, (2013). *Resident Coordinator's Annual Report: Mauritius and Seychelles.*

Cleary, and McConville, (2006). *The need for Good Governance in Multi-Ethnic Societies: The Case of Mauritius.* World Journal ofSocial Sciences; vol. 2, No 7.

Johnson, R. W. (2010). *Decentralization and Structural Adjustment in Africa.*

Johnson, R. W. (2010). *Analyzing decentralization resource regions from a polycentric perspective.*

Chaudhry, S. (1993). *Public management in developing countries: from downsizing to governance; Public management.* An International Journal of Research and Theory.

Olowu, D. (1999). *Decentralization and poverty reduction in Africa: The policy of local – central Relations;* vol. 23, issue 1.

Dodoo, R. (1996). *Lessons from the new public management in Commonwealth nations.* International Public Management Journal. Vol. 1 issue 1.

World Bank, (1997). *Reforming dysfunctional institutions through democratization? Reflection on Ghana:* Journal of Modern African Studies; Cambridge University Press, vol. 35, issue 4.

UN, (2005). Ghana: *Democracy, Economic Reform and Development. Journal of Sustainable Development in Africa;* vol. 14, No 1.

Maravic, P. (2009). *The African Governance Crisis: Improving Public Administration in Africa; a policy analysis.*

Tiruneh, G. (2004). *Is Botswana the Miracle of Africa? Democracy, the Rule of Law, and Human Rights versus Economic Development.* Transnational Law and Contemporary Problems. Vol. 19.

An African Success Stories, (2001). *Explaining Botswana's Success: The Critical Role to Post-colonial Policy.* The social science research network.

Olmstead, P. (2004). *Is Botswana the Miracle of Africa: Democracy, the rule of law, and human rights versus economicdevelopment.*Transnational law and con temporary problems; vol. 19:453.

McGreal, C. (2013). Nelson Mandela: *How Africa has changed in his life time.* The Guardian news and media limited.

Africa Report, (2013). *Burkina Faso's West African Spring:* Democracy and Governance; the Agence France-Press.

University World News,(2010). *The Global Window on Higher Education;* issue No 377.

UNDP, (2009). *Owning the participatory process in Burkina Faso:* UNDP supports decentralization and community-level decision-making.

Journal of Public Administration and Development, (2010). *Local government discretion and accountability in Burkina Faso;* vol. 30, issue 5.

World Bank, (2013). *Second phase of the community based rural development project;* Country's report #: 78591 vol.1.

Marian, L. (2012). *Ethiopia Country Report: Transforming the Democratic and Reform Process;* www.bti-protect.org.

Kenya, (1999). *The Challenges of Governance, Public Sector Reform and Public Administration in Africa.* The DPMN Bulletin: vol. x, # 3.

Taylor/USAID, (2014). *Senegal: Democracy and Governance Fact Sheet/ UnitedStates Agency for International Development;* Country Report.

Journal of Public Administration and Development, (2010*). Local government discretion and accountability in Burkina Faso;* vol.30, issue 5.

World Bank, (2013). *Second Phase of the Community-based Rural Development project;* report # 78591 vol. 1.

Kenya, (1999). *The Challenges of Governance, Public Sector Reform and Public Administration in Africa.* The DPMN Bulletin: vol. # 3.

IMF, (2012). *Press Release: IMF Executive Board Country Report;* www. IMF.org/external/country/NGA.

Library of Congress, (2008). *Country profile: Federal Republic of Nigeria; federal Research Division.*

Martin, (2013). *Rethinking the Ideas of Pan-Africanism and African Unity: Kwame Nkrumah's Leadership Trait Analysis.* The Journal of Pan African Studies, vol. 6, no. 6.

Danabo, P. (2008). *Pan-Africanism and African Unity: From ideal to Practice. www.palgraveconnect.com.*

Muiu, M. W. & Martin, G. (2009). *Region-building in Africa: Political and Economic Challenges. Center for Conflict Resolution (CCR), Cape Town, South Africa.*

Han, M. (2008) &Murithi, T. (2009). *The African Union as a Security Actor: African Solution to African problems.*

Lindeke, W. A. (1995). *Human Rights and Democratic Transition in Namibia: Critical New Representatives.* Indiana University Press; vol.43, no. 4

UNDP, (2003).*Political Culture and Democratic Governance in Southern Africa*. African Journal of political Science. Michigan State University Library

Hochschild, A. (1998). *State Crime in the Heart of Darkness:* Oxford University Press. Vol. 45, issue 4.

Gazibo, M. (2012). *Beyond Electoral Democracy: Foreign Aid and the Challenge of Deepening Democracy in Benin.*

Steward, J. (2012). *Beyond Electoral Democracy: Foreign Aid and the Challenge of Deepening Democracy in Benin.*

Resolution 2145, XXI, (1966). *Liberating Namibia: The Long Diplomatic Struggle between the United Nations and South Africa.* McFarland & Company, Inc., Publishers: Jefferson, North Carolina, and London.

French National Library, (2010). *Music of the Democratic Republic of Congo.* The International information and Library Review. Vol. 36.

French National Library, (2010). *Music of the Democratic Republic of Congo.* From Wikipedia, the free Encyclopedia.

Harvard International Review, (2009). *Back in Business: Sierra Leone's President & CEO: Winning the Fight;* vol. 31, no. 20.

Gumende, A. (2010). Mozambique: *Historic Trajectories and Development.* Hispanic and Research Journal vol. 11.

Schneidman, W. (2004). *Mozambique as Weapons: The Politics of Peace and Silence in Post-Civil War in Mozambique.* Journal of Southern Africa Studies. Vol. 34, no 3.

Hall, M. & Young, T. (1997). *Confronting Leviathan: Mozambique since Independence.* The International Journal of African Historical Studies. Vol. 33, no 1.

Lansner, T. R. (2015). *After a Democratic Power Transfer, Zambia must tackle Chinese Investment Issues and Human Rights Reforms.* The Freedom House Country Report.

IMF, (2012). *Nigeria's Rebased Economy and its Role in Regional and Global Politics.* E-International Relations IMF Country Report.

Maravic, V. (2009). *Implementing a Revenue Authority Model of Tax Administration.* SAGE Publication Journals.

African Democracy, (2012). *African Democracy: A Glass Half-full*. The Economist News Magazine.

Mohan, G. (2002). *The Shape of Sociology for the 21ˢᵗ Century: Tradition and Renewal*. The SAGE Publication Journals.

Muiu, M. W. & Martin, G. (2009). *Region-building in Africa: Political and Economic Challenges*. Journal of African and Asian Studies.

Maffei, W. @007). *The European as a model of African Union*. University of Miami.

Kaba, A.J. (2004). *African Development in the Era of Barack Obama: The Role of the African Union*. The Journal of Pan African Studies, vol. 2, no 9.

Kofman, D. (2007). *Why can't they make an African Union like the European Union?* Quora, Inc. Mountain View, California.

Kaba, A. J. (2007); Wisner, et al. (2005). *From Pan-Africanism to the Union of Africa;* Global Policy Forum Report.

Third World Quarterly Report, (2006). *Conflict and Peace–building in the African Great Lakes Region;* Indiana University Press: Bloomington, Indiana.

Bernard, et al.; (2008). *Civil Society; Public Action and Accountability in Africa:* The Harvard Kennedy School of Government; the Faculty Research Working Paper Series.

Mpepo, B. and Schamani, D. (2005). *Civil Society Participation in Governance Reform Process and Poverty Reduction in Zambia*. The Academic.edu report. From Wikipedia, the Free Encyclopedia.

INDEX

C

CABRI (African Budget Institute), 53

Cameroon
    as authoritarian regime, 50
    as beginner/nonstarter, 50

Cao, Diogo, 119

Cape Verde Islands
    African Party for the Independence
        of Guinea-Bissau and Cape
        Verde (PAIGC), 63–64
    as full democracy, 49
    overview, 63–64
    success case of political reform,
        64–66

Catholic Justice and Peace Commission
    (CFC), 144

CBOs (community-based
    organizations), 21

Cease-Fire Monitoring Group
    (ECOMOG), 144

Center for Budget Advocacy (CBA), 37

Center for Law and Human Rights
    Education (CLHRE), 144

Central African Republic, as beginner/
    nonstarter, 50

Chad, as authoritarian regime, 50

Charm, Abdulair Hamid, 136

Chiluba, Frederick, 147

China
    involvement of in Africa, 15, 16,
        17–18
    Zambian-Chinese Agenda,
        148–150

Christmas War, 90

civil service
    reduction in, 58
    rehabilitation efforts, 44–45
    salaries in, 58

civil society
    accountability and, 23–24, 26–27
    defined, according to World
        Bank, 21

described, 21
    history of in Africa, 22
    role of, 21–27, 62, 73, 74–75, 91,
        95–96, 106–107, 143–144
    USAID partnership with in
        Tanzania, 79–80

Civil Society Coalition for Quality
    Basic Education (CSQBE), 36

Civil Society for Poverty Reduction
    (SCPR), 36

civil society organizations (CSOs), 24,
    25, 26, 27, 35, 36, 39, 60, 79, 97,
    135, 143, 144

civil unrest, 28, 147

Cleary, Dennis, 55

CLHRE (Center for Law and Human
    Rights Education), 144

Clinton, Bill, 8, 18

colonialism
    experiencing of, 84
    impact of, 109
    as legacy of mismanagement, 9
    resistance to, 98–99
    reworking of post-World War II,
        83–86
    transition from, 83

committed reformers, 49, 57

common currency, 2, 43

Commonwealth Foundation, 25

communication, impact of technology
    on, 48

Community of Sahel-Saharan
    States, 90

community-based organizations
    (CBOs), 21

Comoros Islands, as authoritarian
    regime, 50

Compaoré, Blaise, 89, 90

CONAKAT party, 124, 125

conflict resolution
    in Casamance region
        (Senegal), 104

K

Kaba, Amadu Jacky, 9, 19
Kabasele, Joseph (Grand Kalle), 129
Kabila, Laurent-Desire, 128
Kagame, Paul, 131
Kalle, Pepe, 130
Kanda Bongo Man, 130
Kanyatta, Jomo, 2, 99
Kargbo, John Abdul, 134–135
Katanga state, origins of, 124–128
Kaunda, Kenneth, 81, 148
Keefer, Philip, 38
Keita, Modibo, 2
Kenya
    challenges of after independence,
      99–100
    challenges to good governance in,
      101–102
    elections in, 47, 102
    as flawed democracy, 49
    Mau Mau rebellion, 86
    overview, 98–99
    strengthening integrity and
      accountability in, 98–99
    village organizations in, 39
Kenya Economic Survey, 99, 100
Kenyan Demographic and Health
    Survey, 100
Kerekou, Mathieu, 112
Khama, Seretse, 80
Khemani, Stuti, 38
Kikwee, Jakaya, 102
Kimathi, Dedan, 99
Kofman, D., 7
Kolosory, Antoine Wendo, 129
Konaré, Alpha Omar, 115
Koroma, Ernest Bai, 136, 137
Kurylo, Anastacia, 7

L

La Francophonie, 90
Lansner, Thomas, 149

LCC (Liberia Council of
    Churches), 143
Leadership Code, 76, 77
League of Nations, 84, 118
Learning Management System
    (LMS), 55
Leith, J. Clark, 63
Leopold II (king), 124
Lewis, Stephen, 63
Liberia
    as beginner/nonstarter, 50
    elections in, 45–46
    as having reputable if imperfect
      political systems, 47
    humanist capitalism in, 70
    leadership in, 48, 70
    role of civil society in post-conflict
      Liberia, 143–144
    role of youth in, 144–145
    single-party rule in, 64
    Total Involvement for Higher
      Heights, 70
    youth development programs in,
      145–147
Liberia Council of Churches
    (LCC), 143
Liberian Truth and Reconciliation
    Commission (TRC), 89
Liberian Women's Initiative (LWI), 144
Libya
    Burkina Faso's ties with, 90
    effect of on Tunisia, 71
    as hybrid regime, 50
    youth involvement in, 26
Liua, Lipua, 130
LMS (Learning Management
    System), 55
Lome Summit, 5
London Missionary Society, 119
Longomba, Vicky, 130
Lumumba, Patrice, 2, 34, 124,
    125, 126
Lungu, 150

R

radio programming, impact of, 38
Rajaonarimampianina, Hery, 46
Rajoelina, Andre, 46
reconstruction, peace building and, 28, 30, 141
regional cooperation, need for efforts to promote/strengthen, 43
René, France, 70
Robeson, Paul, 1
Robinson, James A., 63
Rochereau, Tabu Ley, 130
rock-rumba, 129
romanticism, 1
Rotberg, Robert, 19, 20
rumba, 129, 130
Rwanda
    conflicts in, 31–32
    as flawed democracy, 49
    genocide in, 39
    peace making initiative, 33
    reforming economy of, 130–133
    role of women in, 133–134
Rwanda Women Parliamentarians Forum, 133
Rwandan Utilities and Regulatory Agency, 132

S

SADC (Southern African Development Community), 25, 80
SADCC (Southern African Development Coordination Conference), 80
Samatar, Abdi, 63
San (Bushmen, Basarwa), 61–62, 119
Sandinistas, 90
Sankara, Thomas, 89, 90
Sao Tomé, elections in, 64
Sata, Michael, 147, 148, 149, 150
Savimbi, Jonas, 87
Schneidman, Witney, 140

Scot, Guy, 150
SCPR (Civil Society for Poverty Reduction), 36
secret ballots, 47
sectionalism, 58
Security Council Resolution 161, 126
Security Council Resolution 435, 120
SEEDS (State Economic Empowerment Development Strategy), 110
Selassie, Haile, 2
self-determination, 47, 85
Senegal
    democracy in, 103–104
    democratic tradition in, 45
    as flawed democracy, 49
    political developments in, 48
    proliferation of village organizations in, 39
    reforms and democratic transformations in, 64
Seychelles
    challenges for, 69–70
    electoral process in, 69
    as full democracy, 49
    overview, 66–67
    as parable of success, 67–69
ShamaShama, 130
Sierra Leone
    challenges in, 137–138
    elections in, 48
    as flawed democracy, 49
    good governance, democratic reform, and accountability in, 134–137
    as having reputable if imperfect political systems, 47
Sirleaf, Ellen Johnson, 143
Sirte Declaration, 5
Sirte Extraordinary Session, 5
Sisulu, Walter, 85
social accountability
    defined, 26–27
    driving forces behind, 27